Broke

Secrets to Fix America's Financial Crisis

"For we are God's masterpiece. He created us anew in Christ Jesus, so we can do the good things he planned for us long ago."
Ephesians 2:10

Broke

Secrets to Fix America's Financial Crisis

DAKOTA GRADY

Published by Upstate Essential Solutions, LLC.
Greenville, South Carolina 29616

This book is created to give accurate and authoritative information with regard to personal finance and the other topics discussed. It is sold understanding that the publisher is not providing financial, accounting, investing, or other professional advice. If financial or other professional expertise is needed, it is recommended to seek help from a competent professional.

Scripture quotations marked NLT are taken from the *Holy Bible*, New Living Translation, copyright © 1996, 2004. Used by permission of Tyndale House Publishers, Inc., Carol Stream, Illinois 60188. All rights reserved.

Editor: Dakota Grady
Cover Design: Abeebzy & Naeemkhan33
Back Photograph: Marcus Whitner

ISBN: 978-1-7326059-2-3

Contents

Contents

Dedication

I want to dedicate this book to my wife, Shameka Nicole. Thank you for loving me even when I don't deserve it.

Acknowledgements

First, I want to thank my Savior, Jesus Christ. Lord thank you for rising for me. I am rising for you. To Naomi: You're God's gift to us!

Thank you to all of the people that have supported me on this journey.

Preface

For you to understand this book, I think understanding my story will give you, the reader, a perspective about this journey. My story began in Greenville, South Carolina, my hometown. I grew up in a large family. My parents had seven children; six boys and one girl (my mother had two sets of twins!). We were like the *Brady Bunch*, but we were the "Grady Bunch" (our last name is Grady). My mother and father did not earn a lot of money. My dad worked in manufacturing plants, while my mother worked at a dry cleaner. In fact, we lived in a low-income neighborhood or in "the hood." We lived in the same neighborhood as Jesse Jackson, Civil Rights activist. We received food stamps from the Federal government because we qualified for federal assistance. I remember getting pieces of paper (i.e., food stamps) that resembled money, only those pieces of paper could only purchase food (not a fancy new car). Although I liked the food that I was able to buy at the local grocery store, I felt so ashamed to be on welfare.

The neighborhood that we lived in was drug, trash, and roach infested. My parents provided us with the necessities and luxuries that we needed and wanted. My siblings and I had the latest video game systems. Children from the neighborhood would come to our apartment to play video games with us. We did not have a lot of money, but we had what we wanted. Later, my family moved from the "hood" to a different area of town (just a different "hood" but we lived in a house).

When we moved, I was in middle school, and I remember times when we had to use the burner on our stove to heat the iron to iron clothes because the iron needed replacing. There were times when we turned on the oven to heat our house. I remember waking up in the morning to go to the bathroom, and it was so cold; even though I lived in the South, winter weather can be unbearable. One memory remains in my mind that motivates me to continue to pursue my dream. That memory is of a time when my family did not have electricity because it had been disconnected. My parents put all of my siblings and me in the car (I believe the car was a station wagon – only a ship could transport a basketball team and its two coaches) and took us to our grandmother's house. Grandmother (or "grandma") Della Mae Jones, my mother's biological mother, was a big lady with a very kind heart and a love for Jesus and people. Grandma had a fiery oil stove that warmed her entire house. My parents left us at my grandmother's house so that we could stay warm and not have to sleep in a cold house; however, my parents went back to our house. They sacrificed themselves, so that we could be warm. I will probably never forget that moment.

During the summer before going to high school, I got my first job that was part of a training program. I attended an aviation program and got paid for attending. I got a chance to fly an airplane during the program (with the help of a pilot of course) and was able to save money to buy my own clothes. This was the turning point for me regarding money because my parents did not teach me to handle money on purpose. Saving money was a gift that came to me naturally. In high school, I worked at a car wash to earn money. I worked part-time after school, and I saved money to pay for my first car, a 1986 Oldsmobile Cutlass Supreme. I paid cash for the car, well, almost because I still owed the seller $100 for the car, which one of my brothers paid to get the title and since I have never had a car payment (and will NEVER have one!). I worked at a car wash for two and a half years while in school. When I graduated high school, I was the first one in my immediate family to graduate. I enrolled in a technical college to pursue a welding career. I worked a full-time job at a vitamin manufacturer as a material handler/assembly line worker while being a full-time student. I worked and saved money as I had done since starting working.

While attending technical college, my psychology professor, Montina Wesley, saw the potential in me, sort of like a "diamond in the rough." She arranged for me to take an IQ test, which came back with great results. Thereafter, Montina contacted a student assistant program at the technical college and got me connected with Sinclair Williams, an employee of the college's TRIO Program. Sinclair's connection with a college in Kentucky enabled me to learn about the college and the benefits of attending. I applied to the college and was accepted into the college's bachelor program. After completing my associate's degree with the technical college, I began to further my education at the college in Kentucky. By this time, I saved over $2,000 while working and going to school.

I was blessed to attend the college in Kentucky as it focuses on providing people from low-income backgrounds a quality, affordable education. The college's labor program required students to work 10-20 hours per week while pursuing an education. As I worked and studied, I paid my school term bill (i.e., room and board) and graduated in four years with no student loan debt! I only owed about $1,000 for a dental procedure that the college funded.

After graduating college for my bachelor's degree, I moved back home and got a job as an auditor. I audited collection agencies that collected past due credit card debt to ensure that they were doing their jobs properly. I lived with my parents for about five months before renting my own apartment. As an auditor, I got a promotion that allowed me to travel across the United States performing onsite audits of my clients. During this time, I saved about $6,000! Although I earned a decent living, I had a desire to do more to impact other people's lives. In 2007, while working as an auditor, my employer offered tickets to see an event on personal finances. That event was the turning point in my life to help me unlock the passion to help people become financially literate.

At the personal finance event, my eyes and mind were opened to new ways of thinking about money. As I said before, my parents did not teach me about money, so I was ignorant in many areas of personal finance. The event gave me the tools to enhance my gift of smart money management. With this new knowledge and a passion to help other people become empowered with their personal finances, I started coaching people in 2010.

After getting married in 2008, I found out that Shameka, my new wife, had debt. She owed more money than I had ever owed! Her debt became my debt (that's right, you become "one" when you say, "I do"). We owed in excess of *$38,000* for a car, old medical bills, student loans, and for rental fees an apartment that my wife rented before we got married. Shameka and I made a plan to eliminate the debt. We were able to settle (i.e., pay a reduced amount) a lot of the debt for pennies on the dollar. The car loan that we owed was about $26,000, but we were able to settle it for about $2,000!

In December 2013, we paid off about $20,000 of debt to become debt free! Becoming debt free gave us hope. Hope for a better financial future. The journey was very hard, but worth the fight. In 2015 I started the Dream Chaser Group as a financial coach to help people become empowered through financial literacy. I wanted to share this message with other people because people need hope every day, everywhere. When people have their "financial houses" in order, they have the potential to chase their dreams (hence the name The Dream Chaser Group).

Your debt load may be $200, $2,000, or $200,000; no matter how many zeros there are you can overcome being broke. If you apply the principles that follow in these pages to your life, you will not be broke. It will not be easy, but the process is worthwhile. Are you ready for a better life and a brighter financial future? If so then let's get started!

Introduction
Time to Stop Being Broke – Level Up

What exactly is hope? Hope is something that fuels you to strive for a dream that goes beyond your human ability to achieve. Hope is the fire that burns deep within you when your life is full of darkness. It is a feeling of desire for an outcome that may seem unobtainable, but is within reach. Hope is the feeling that what is wanted can be had or that events will turn out for the best.[1] Hope is a desire to live another day when you feel like giving up; hope is never quitting despite the odds or fear of failure. Hope motivates, inspires, and encourages when situations seem hopeless.

Broke will give you hope for a prosperous financial future that enables people to chase AND catch their dreams and live a life of independence from financial bondage and hopelessness. This book not only frees you financially; it will enhance the communication in your marriage, strengthen relationships with other people, relieve you from emotional stress, allow you to improve your physical health, and give you the boldness to live a life of purpose. That is the power of Broke! It has the tools to help you transform your life if you are ready AND willing to change.

Broke will give you a path to financial success. As I said earlier, the process is not easy to achieve, but the results will be worthwhile. Financial freedom is available to anyone seeking to improve their financial future. The keys to success include hard work, determination, perseverance, discipline, sacrifice, and behavior change.

The most important ingredient is YOU! This process will not work unless you are willing to work! If you are tired of living paycheck to paycheck, then get ready for the ride to maximize your money and stop being broke! Lastly, throughout the book there are references to the Bible. As a follower of Jesus Christ, I strive to lead people to handle money wisely. These principles of smart money management can work for everyone regardless of their faith.

I want to make one last point before we get started. There are other financial experts (past and present) teaching or who have taught people about money. You may see something in this book that you have heard before. I have used the principles that others have developed and created a process to help people handle money on purpose using similar principles, but a different way of presenting them.

Ready to Take Your Money and Life to the Next Level!

Your Money Academy is the premier personal finance course to help you go from where you are to where you want to be financially. In this 7-week course, Dakota Grady will teach you about:

Budgeting

Debt Elimination

Saving (College, Home Buying, & Unexpected Events)

Retirement

Wealth Accumulation

Money Management

Register at Dakotagrady.com

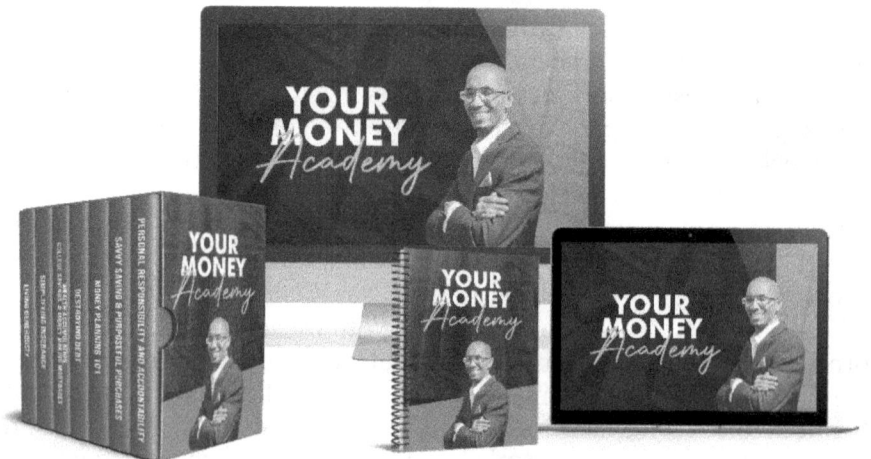

Part I
The Foundation
1
The Rainy Day Fund: Umbrella for the Unpredictable
The $1.5K Sprint: Do it FAST!

Have you ever prepared to run a race such as a 5k or marathon? I have never run a marathon, but I hear that it takes discipline and hard work. Anything worth doing takes those two elements. I remember when I was growing up in South Carolina, and we would have to run a mile for gym class. I was not a runner as a child, so I struggled to finish the one mile run because I did not condition myself to run regularly. I remember the inside of my chest burning because I did not run consistently, so I paid the price physically. Have you ever felt that burning feeling?

If you want to win at anything in life, it takes discipline. Winning with money is no different. Discipline is something that everyone needs. You may have discipline in one area of your life, but not in other areas. For me, I am disciplined with money. Handling it wisely comes naturally to me. However, I am not disciplined in getting sleep (actually I am awake at 2:30 a.m. writing this book!). To begin this journey to maximize your money to stop being broke, discipline is a major component of the process. Without it, you will not move toward a financial future that you desire. Discipline is an integral part of developing habits that will benefit you in the long run. What is discipline? Discipline is an activity, exercise, or a regimen that develops a skill.[1] It also involves doing the task over time with consistency and perseverance. Here's an example. Writing a book takes discipline. You must be committed to the process of brainstorming, outlining, researching, editing, and scheduling time to write the book. You have to conquer writer's block, which is actually overcome by having an outline, and you will have to overcome other distractions that could take your focus off of the goal. With discipline, writing a book can become a reality. Following the principles of Broke requires discipline as well.

As you prepare for the journey, there will be obstacles that hinder you from moving along the path. Unexpected events will occur that may cause you to lose focus. That is why discipline is critical because you will encounter distractions as you pursue your dreams of a better financial future. But when unexpected events do occur, you will be ready to stay on track and not falter.

1

Rain, Rain, Go Away. Come Again Another Day

In life there will be times of "rainy days" or unexpected events that cause pain, heartache, and hurt. These events may have a major impact on you, your family, and your plan. No one is exempt from life's challenges and trials, but you can anticipate road blocks as you navigate on your journey. Terry Felber, author of *The Legend of the Monk and the Merchant*, said "See challenges as stepping stones, not as obstacles."[2] You can PLAN for the unexpected events that life gives you. Unexpected events happen and being prepared for them is part of the foundation of Broke.

Several unexpected events have happened to me on my journey of smart money management. Even smart people have rainy days. In August 2008, I was awake early one morning (just like now), and I was using the computer when I heard a strange noise outside of my apartment. I looked out the window, but did not notice anything suspicious. I continued what I was doing. Later that morning as I was going to my car to go to work at my full-time job, I did not see my car in the parking lot. My wife had already left for work. I called her and said, "Honey, have you seen my car?" "No," she said. Then, I looked down at the ground and saw broken glass. At that moment, I realized what had happened. "Man, somebody stole my car," I said. The car was a 1985 Oldsmobile Delta 88; the car was so large it looked like the Titanic. I had just bought new rotors and brakes for my car, which were lying on the floor of my car, AND I left money in the glove compartment. (Word of wisdom: Never leave money in the glove compartment of your car). Someone wanted my car more than I did; I called the police to file a report and called my job as well to inform my supervisor of the incident. Fortunately, I had $1,000 saved in my Rainy Day Fund to replace my car. An acquaintance was selling a 1996 Toyota Corolla. I contacted her about the car, and my brother Jeff and I went to view and drive the car. After a very long negotiation, which I will discuss later in the book, I was able to buy the car for $900 cash. I even had money left to purchase insurance for the car. Later I replenished my $1,000 Rainy Day Fund. Life is good when you can pay cash for a car and not go into debt.

Another example of how a Rainy Day Fund can relieve the stress of unexpected events was when my wife and I lived in Oklahoma. In August 2012, Shameka, my wife, relocated to Oklahoma City for a job as a maintenance technician that she accepted after college. We planned to live apart for a year so that I could further my education and get work experience in accounting; my wife would live in Oklahoma, while I would live in South Carolina (not a smart plan). We loaded most of our furniture and other belongings into a truck and drove half way across the United States to Oklahoma. We towed her car, the 1996 Toyota Corolla, with us. We drove through Atlanta, Georgia, Birmingham, Alabama, Tupelo,

Mississippi, and Little Rock, Arkansas. Arkansas's long stretch of farm land does not make for a scenic route to Oklahoma. After driving more than twelve hours, we arrived in Oklahoma City!

The next day, we were given the keys to the apartment and unloaded the furniture and the Toyota Corolla. We needed to unload items quickly and return the moving truck and trailer, as my plane flight back to South Carolina departed later that day. After unloading and returning the truck and trailer, my wife drove me to the airport in Oklahoma City. We said our good byes with many tears as we left each other. And, I flew back to South Carolina. Then, after one month of separation we decided that I would move to Oklahoma City as well. I admit being separated from her was difficult and could have been detrimental to our marriage; however, we wanted to remain married. In September 2012, I reunited with my bride.

Then, later that year, an unexpected event happened. My wife's Toyota Corolla had not been operating properly. We had our mechanic check it and replace the transmission fluid. We were going home from the mechanic's shop after the repair, and as I was driving on the interstate the transmission stopped working. We had to have the car towed to our apartment. I did not expect the transmission to stop working; although, a previous mechanic identified transmission issues prior to the mishaps. I just did not believe him; there's a reason that he is a mechanic and I am not.

We sold the Toyota Corolla and added the money to our Rainy Day Fund to purchase another car. Then, we bought a Mazda Millennia from an auction, which was a stupid buying decision because the car was a "lemon." The lights did not work properly, and it had electrical issues; eventually, we sold the lemon and saved more money for another car purchase. (Word of wisdom: Never buy a car from an auction).

Finally, we were able to save $3,500 to buy a new "used" car. I searched online and found a 1999 Honda Accord. The seller wanted more than we had to spend; I showed the seller the money that we had to spend, but he was not willing to sell at the requested price. I walked away. Cash gives you the power to walk away from a purchase if no bargain is offered. Then, the seller called me back and offered to sell the car to me for $3,500! By having money in our Rainy Day Fund, we were able to remove the stress of having to finance a vehicle.

Even though we prepared for the unexpected, Shameka and I still experienced the "rain." Most of our experiences with the "rain" have been with automobiles. This story is no different. In September 2013, Shameka and I still lived in Oklahoma, but had moved to Midwest City, Oklahoma, a city near Oklahoma City. We planned to relocate to Tennessee to live closer to family in South Carolina and to move away from the treacherous tornadoes. (I never experienced the effects of a tornado until moving to Oklahoma).

My wife had already accepted a job in Nashville, Tennessee, and I diligently searched for work in the same area. One particular September evening, the parking spaces were full of cars where I normally parked my car. Therefore, I parked my car on the side of the apartment complex, so I could not see it from my apartment. The next morning, I went to my car to go to work (de se vu all over again), and when I tried to start my car it would not start. I saw that some of my belongings in the car had been moved from their usual places. Then, I looked at the ignition switch and saw that it was destroyed. I realized that someone tried to steal my car (again). This time, the thief did not succeed. I contacted the police to file a report and an officer came to the apartment complex to gather evidence for an investigation. What did I do? I replaced my ignition switch, AND I installed an alarm on my car. The Rainy Day Fund came in handy during a time of crisis.

Learn to Dance in the Rain

Why have a Rainy Day Fund? Well, if you are not convinced yet, here are other reasons to save for the unexpected in your life. Ever lost a job? I have, several times. I lost three jobs the first three years living in Tennessee. Because we had a Rainy Day Fund, my wife and I were able to weather the storms of job losses.

We were prepared. How? We had a Rainy Day Fund. Are there other reasons to have a Rainy Day Fund? Major medical issue or disability due to a job related injury are examples of unexpected events that could happen. Sometimes in life it rains, and when it does a Rainy Day Fund will be your umbrella.

Now that you know "Why" a Rainy Day Fund is important, here is "How" you save for a Rainy Day Fund. The first step to get a Rainy Day Fund is to decide to save money. If you do not make a decision to save money, it will not happen. Saving money must be a priority. Once you decide, the next step is to save $500 - $1,500 for your mini Rainy Day Fund. Put $500 - $1,500 in a savings account, which is a type of account that allows you to get your money if needed. You can put the money in a savings account at a bank or credit union. The Rainy Day Fund is insurance against life's unexpected events. It will be like you are running a sprint because you need to save $500 - $1,500 as quickly as possible! You can do it! Get started NOW!

How do you save $500 - $1,500 really, really fast? You could do the following to save for your Rainy Day Fund:

- Work overtime at your job
- Get a part-time job in addition to your full-time job
- Sell items in your home that are not being used
- Start a part-time business to earn extra money
- Reduce your lifestyle (e.g., stop going to restaurants for a short period of time or terminate your monthly cable television subscription -- yes, I said turn off your cable TV!)
- Use coupons to reduce your grocery bill

You can get creative to make more money to save for your Rainy Day Fund. Having a Rainy Day Fund will reduce the worry and stress concerning unexpected events. Shameka and I have a Rainy Day Fund, and it has been a life line for our finances and marriage. In my experience in having this money saved for the "rain," once you get and keep a Rainy Day Fund, life's unexpected events are far and few. Try it, and you will see how it will improve your financial life.

According to research, 39% of Americans can pay for a $1,000 emergency expense.[3] That means that more than 60% of Americans could not cover the cost of a $1,000 unexpected event. Don't be part of the 60% of people that get wet by the rain.

Action Steps to Maximize Your Money to Stop Being Broke
Getting knowledge is great! But knowledge without application does not add value to your life or to others. In his book, *How to Win Friends and Influence People*, Dale Carnegie quoted Herbert Spencer saying, "The great aim of education is not knowledge but action."[4] Broke is a book about action; your life will not change unless you change. Action is part of change. Here are some action steps to help you apply what you have learned.

1. Are you convinced that a Rainy Day Fund is important? If so, set a goal to save $500 - $1,500 by a specific date. For example, your goal could be: "I will save $1,500 for my mini Rainy Day Fund within the next two months." (If you are not convinced of the importance of a Rainy Day Fund, why aren't you persuaded? I challenge you to save the money and see if your financial life improves regarding unexpected events).
2. Now that you have set your goal, how are you going save the money? Are you going to sell something, work overtime, or get a part-time job?
3. Lastly, open a savings account to deposit the money for your mini Rainy Day Fund.

Money Planning 101
The Foundational Element

My wife and I were married on March 22, 2008. We will be celebrating our tenth wedding anniversary next year; however, the journey before the wedding was challenging. In fact, we got married on our third attempt. We had some issues before we got married. Before the wedding though, we planned. That's right. We planned to get married. Shameka and I planned a traditional wedding. We discussed the location of our wedding, honeymoon, wedding party participants, food, and all of the other details that make a wedding happen.

Part of our planning included attending pre-marital counseling with her Bishop Gregory Carter. Shameka and I went to two counseling sessions, and Bishop Carter shared his wisdom of being married. I remember him saying, "Whether the husband or wife earns the income, it is all 'household' money." That is one thing that I remember from the session. Overall, the sessions were a disaster! Although Shameka and I planned to get married, we had some issues to resolve, especially about personal finance! In fact, we only had two counseling sessions because the bishop was not willing to continue counseling us. Bummer! We must have been very bad counselees. Despite the personal finance issues, Shameka and I were married. My wedding day was one of the best days of my life. After getting married, we had our honeymoon in Savannah, Georgia. The wedding and honeymoon were intentional because we planned.

Plan for Failure or Success, the Choice is Yours

Zig Ziglar, author and motivational speaker, said "Plan to win, prepare to win, and expect to win." Winning starts with planning. After planning, one must prepare; without planning and preparation, one cannot expect to win. What area of your life do you want to win? Do you want to win in your career, marriage, relationships, parenting, health, or finances? It all starts with a plan. Once you have a plan, you must execute the plan. Planning is the foundation of winning in life. Benjamin Franklin said, "If you fail to plan, you are planning to fail." After the plan has been established you must take action to make the plan happen.

For example, if you want a marvelous marriage, you must be intentional by planning and executing the plan. Communicate with your spouse on a regular basis. Go eat at your favorite restaurant once or twice a month with your mate. Attend festivals, concerts, volunteer, and do many other fun, relaxing, and rejuvenating activities with your spouse to make your marriage great.

Do you want to lose weight? Set a goal that is specific, measurable, attainable, make it relevant to you, set a time limit, and put it in writing. If you say, "I want to lose weight." That goal is vague, and you probably will not attain it because it does not include the elements mentioned above. However, if you say, "I want to lose 60 pounds in three months," you will more than likely reach your goal because it is specific, measurable, attainable, relevant, and has a time limit. Now that goal gives you a target to aim at. Let's break that goal down by each element.

First, the goal is specific; losing sixty pounds. It is measurable and attainable. You can lose twenty pounds each month, and the goal is relevant to you. It's YOUR goal, not someone else's goal for you and there is a time limit, which is three months. Lastly, put your goal in writing. Post the goal somewhere you can see it; review your goal often to keep you focused on achieving it. When your goal has those elements, executing the plan becomes easier. Make sure your plan (whether it's for weight loss, career change, relationship development, or any other area of your life) is designed for a successful execution.

Plan for Your Money

An old Proverb tells followers of Christ to plan. It says, "Do your planning and prepare your fields before building your house."[1] I consider myself a planner; as a follower of Christ, I would be wise to plan. As I mentioned before, Shameka and I planned our wedding and honeymoon. We set a plan to have a great wedding and honeymoon and executed the plan. However, we did not plan to have a marvelous marriage. In fact, according to the Wall Street Journal, money was the number one point of conflict in the majority of marriages studied by Dr. Terri Orbuch, a psychologist and researcher at the University of Michigan. Forty-nine percent of divorced people from her study said they fought so much over money with their spouse.[2]

If money is the number [one] problem that causes divorce, wouldn't it be wise to have a plan for your money in your marriage? If money fights is the number one problem in a marriage, this area can also be the number one area that can heal marriages. It is imperative that you and your spouse work as a team to create a plan for your money. What kind of plan do you need? You need a Monthly Money Plan.

Why create a Monthly Money Plan, or budget? Well, if you are married, having a budget will increase the intimacy between you and your spouse. It will heal your marriage and reduce many of the money fights that plague marriages. Budgeting also will increase the communication in your marriage because when you budget it forces communication to occur organically; you and your mate will begin to talk about your fears and dreams regarding money. Both of you will begin to set goals and dream about things that have probably been pushed to the back burner of your lives. A budget is more than about money; it is about enhancing your relationships, especially your marriage.

I have not forgotten about the single people. Singles need to do a budget as much as married couples. Singles need accountability in their lives, and the Money Plan can provide financial accountability. For example, a single man may think that he deserves to spend money that he has worked hard to earn. He may have worked hard for his money, but if he does not have a budget and someone to hold him accountable for his spending, he may very well overspend because he thinks he is entitled to buy things he cannot afford. A budget will empower a single person to make responsible financial decisions. In addition, having an accountability partner adds another layer of accountability for a single person and will help the single person stay on track to make wise financial choices.

Why Create a Money Plan?

What is the "Why" behind creating a Monthly Money Plan? According to Career Builder, "78% of U.S. workers live paycheck to paycheck."[3] That means about eight out of ten Americans are struggling financially. In my opinion, there is a reason that so many people experience financial woes. Here is the reason: According to Gallup, "Nearly one in three Americans prepare a detailed written household budget each month that tracks their income and expenses."[4] Only 33% of Americans budget monthly. That is the reason that people are living paycheck to paycheck. Do you want to be part of those statistics? If not, that is your "Why." Creating a Monthly Money Plan results in many benefits and adds value to different areas of your life.

Financial

A Money Plan will help you get control of your spending and will provide you financial security because it empowers you to handle money intentionally. Having control of your money allows you to achieve the financial goals you desire to accomplish. Money Planning gives you the freedom to save, invest, spend, and accumulate wealth on purpose, so that you can reach your dreams.

Emotional

Money Planning affects your emotional well-being, too. Budgeting reduces the emotional stress caused by poor money management. Imagine being able to feel free from worry because you know where each dollar of your money is being spent, instead of worrying where it went. The value added to your emotional life is priceless.

Physical

The physical benefits of Money Planning can do wonders for you. When you have control of your finances through budgeting, your mind and body relax. Budgeting not only gives you peace of mind, but it gives you the freedom to take care of your body as you should.

Relational

Budgeting enhances the intimacy in marriages as it leads to more communication – communication about fears, goals, and dreams (individual and shared dreams for both spouses). When communication increases in marriage, spouses connect on a deeper level and are able to work together in unity and combat a major cause of divorce in North America – money fights.

Spiritual

Money Planning enables you to connect with God and become more like Him in giving and money management, or stewardship. Budgeting puts in perspective that we are managers of the financial resources entrusted to us and allows us to align ourselves in a manner that honors God.

What Is a Money Plan?

Now that you know the why of budgeting and the benefits it offers, it is time to know what a budget is. Budgeting is simply a plan for your money; hence, a Money Plan. If you do not have a plan for your money, you will not have any money. It's that simple. No plan, no money. Money Planning lets you control where your money is spent, saved, invested, or blown (that's right, money is made to use for fun!). Specifically, I am talking about a "zero-based" Money Plan. A zero-based Money Plan, or budget, gives you the ability to assign each dollar of your income a task or job. For example, when you go to work your boss assigns you a task or project, and you complete that task. Well, you are the boss of your money, and you must make your money behave like it should; so by budgeting you are assigning each dollar of income a task or job to do for you. You are making your money work for you. You are the owner and boss of YOU, Incorporated, and your income is your employee. You get to tell your money what to do and where it should go.

Assign each dollar of your monthly income to certain categories that you spend each month until each dollar is "spent" on paper, intentionally. Once all income is given a "job" or "task", add all of the categories, and subtract the sum total of the categories from your monthly income. The result should be "zero", meaning you budgeted each dollar of your income; therefore, you are living within your means.

Money Planning must be done each month before the next month begins. For example, today is the 22nd, of the month, so I have to do next month's budget before this month ends because I need a plan before the next month starts. Money Planning should be done every month for the rest of your life. No exceptions. If you want to become wealthy and not be broke, doing a Monthly Money Plan will focus your efforts. According to Thomas Stanley, author of *The Millionaire Next Door,* "The foundation stone of wealth accumulation is defense, and this defense should be anchored by budgeting and planning."[5]

Budgeting for Life

I have been budgeting consistently since 2007. I cannot fathom NOT doing a monthly budget. Money Planning is a discipline and habit that I am fond of and will do for the rest of my life. Budgeting has affected me in major ways. By budgeting regularly, Shameka and I communicate more about our monthly income and expenses. In fact, we talk very often, and I attribute that to the Money Plan.

Budgeting has helped us during good and bad times. It has guided us through job losses, relocations, and other life changes like child birth and continuing education. As mentioned earlier in the chapter, Money Planning is the foundation to wealth accumulation. It does not matter how much money you earn; what matters is how well you mange what you earn. Whether you earn $1,000 a month or $100,000 a year, you need a plan for your money. If you want to succeed and win with money, budgeting is the vehicle to lead you to the winner's circle. Preparing your Monthly Money Plan will take time. Do you remember learning to ride a bike or swim for the first time? Were you good at swimming the first time? Absolutely not! I know I struggled to learn to swim. Learning to budget will take practice as well. After about three months, or ninety days, preparing your Monthly Money Plan will improve. So do not be too hard on yourself; give yourself some grace. With practice and repetition, budgeting will become second nature to you. You can do this!

If you are married, I want you to meet with your spouse and discuss some of your dreams and goals. Discuss the chapter and some of your fears about budgeting. Be open and honest with each other. Remember: You and your spouse are a team. The Monthly Money Plan is a tool to help you and your spouse become unified in achieving your financial goals and dreams. So do not let the budget become a tool to control each other. You and your spouse are the bosses of the money, so make it behave. Once you and your spouse have talked, follow the Action Steps below to prepare your first Monthly Money Plan.

For my single people, I encourage you to talk about this chapter with your accountability partner. Share your fears concerning budgeting as well as your future aspirations. Then, apply the Action Steps below.

Whether you are married or single, I want you to know that you can do this budgeting process!

Action Steps to Maximize Your Money to Stop Being Broke

1. Review the Monthly Money Plan in the Broke Management Forms section near the end of this book.

2. Get a copy of your bank statement from the previous month. Identify the different categories of income and expense on the bank statement. Use the Monthly Money Plan as a guide to group the expenses on your bank statement.

3. Prepare a Monthly Money Plan using the numbers from the bank statement that you grouped together in Action Step 2. This will allow you to see what you earned and spent in the previous month. Discuss the results with your spouse or accountability partner.

4. Prepare a Monthly Money Plan for the next month. Use the Monthly Money Plan from the previous month to create a new plan. Adjust any areas that you overspent to make your income minus expenses equal zero.

Stopping the Dream Killer
Learning to Crush Debt

For three years, I worked as an auditor for a large debt buyer. My employer bought bad debt, or debt that had been written off by other companies because people did not repay the money borrowed, and placed the debt with collection agencies. The collection agencies received a commission for the debt they collected.

A lot of the debt was credit card debt that companies sold to my employer for pennies on the dollar. As an auditor, I ensured that the collection agencies were following the Federal Fair Debt Collections Practices Act (FDCPA), other policies, and depositing the funds collected into a trust account for my employer. I audited the call volume, debt payment posting in the collection agencies' collection systems, and other procedures. I reported the results of the audits with recommendations for improvement for the collection agencies.

The debt was placed with collection agencies based on the charge off date (i.e., the date the debt was written off). The debt that had an earlier charge off date was placed with certain agencies and older debt placed with other collection agencies specializing in collecting older debt. The older the charge off date, the higher the commission earned by the collection agency because older debt is harder to collect. Nonetheless, the agencies attempted to collect on all debt. My employer also had an internal mortgage collection department to collect delinquent mortgage debt. In addition, my employer collected on medical debt, which had to be collected in a more sensitive approach.

The collection industry is a big business. According to the Congressional Research Service, the revenue of debt collection agencies in the U.S. was $13.4 billion in 2020.[1] I remember auditing collection agencies that had millions of dollars of debt placed with them to collect on behalf of my employer. There were also attorneys that owned collection agencies that dealt with debt accounts that had judgments (meaning, my employer sued a debtor for the balance owed and won a judgment to collect the debt). Attorneys would collect on those accounts on behalf of the debt buyer, and the attorneys earned a commission for debt collected. My employer's debt servicing included sub-prime lending for automobiles as well. Sub-prime loans are loans that have high interest rates because people that apply for the loans do not have a good credit rating. The debt buyer offered high interest rate financing for vehicles to debtors with bad credit through "buy here, pay here" or "tote-the-note" car dealerships. If a debtor missed a car payment, my employer disabled the car (with a device) so that the debtor could not start the car. Imagine if you had a car from a buy here, pay here dealership, and you missed paying your car note. How would you get to work if your car did not start? How would you get your children to daycare without a car?

During my tenure as an auditor, I used a credit card for my travel expenses such as hotel reservations, airfare, rental car, and meals. I submitted an expense report to my employer for reimbursement for my travel expenses. Once I received reimbursement, I paid off my credit card expenses. I did not like owing people money, so I paid off my credit card every month. Then, one day my employer offered discounted tickets to a personal finance event at a local venue in my hometown. At first, I hesitated to attend the event, but then decided to buy a ticket.

At the event, the speaker presented principles about debt. Now that I think about it, it is ironic that a debt buying company such as my employer offered tickets to an event that could have the potential to put my employer out of business with the principles being taught. Nevertheless, my employer sold tickets to the event, and I attended. The event totally changed my views concerning debt. The concept of living debt free was discussed. At that time in my life, I had never heard of living without debt. I used my credit card "responsibly" by paying it off every month. However, there is risk when using debt. What if I lose my job? What if I become disabled? How would I be able to pay my credit card bill if I lost my job or became disabled? Eventually I was convinced to pursue a debt-free lifestyle. However, changing from using debt to not using debt did not happen immediately.

Because using debt was engrained in my mind, making the transition from using credit to using cash took time. It was a process. So eventually I saved enough money to use for my travel expenses instead of using my credit card. Finally, I decided to pay off my credit card, cut it up, and close my account. I made the decision in 2008 and have not used a credit card since. The decision was a game changer in my life. At the time of the personal finance event, Shameka and I were not yet married. I became debt free and saved about $6,000 in a savings account. Then in 2008, Shameka and I got married, and she brought debt into our marriage. We (when you get married, you and your spouse become "one") then had over $30,000 of debt, which included student loans, credit card debt, car loan, and other debt as well. Shameka and I argued about the debt because I wanted to live debt free, which I was *before* I got married, and she wanted to continue doing the things she wanted to do before marriage like go on vacation. As a natural saver, I wanted to save money for the future, and Shameka who is naturally a spender, wanted to spend,

spend, spend. Our natural bents toward money management caused tension in our marriage as well. Luckily, Shameka and I were able to work together to get on the same page about our finances.

Shameka and I agreed to get out of debt. We worked hard to pay off debt. We settled as many debts as possible. A settlement is when you pay less than you owe for a debt because you do not have the money to pay it in full. A lot of the debt was old debt (i.e., debt that is not current and very past due), which gave us the ability to offer settlement amounts. During the debt elimination process, Shameka and I went back to school to further our education, relocated to Oklahoma for a year for work, relocated to Tennessee (which is where we live today), quit jobs, lost jobs, and replaced cars (which is mentioned throughout this book). Finally, after working for almost six years to eliminate debt, in December 2013 Shameka and I became debt free! You too can become free from bondage. Scripture says, "Just as the rich rule the poor, so the borrower is servant to the lender."[2] We decided to get out of debt; you have to decide as well. Let's discuss debt for a moment.

What You May (or May Not) Have Heard About Debt

Before we start this section, let me define "debt." Debt is money owed to a person(s) or entity that needs to be repaid (may include interest). The different kinds of debt include student loans, credit cards, mortgage, auto/vehicle loans, pay day loans, unpaid medical bills, home equity loans (i.e., second mortgage), and personal loans owed to a family member. Most of these loans are debt that you must repay the original amount, plus interest. Interest is what you pay to borrow money; it is the cost of borrowing. Recently, a lady in one of my personal finance classes told me that she did not think of her car note as debt. I told her that the car note is debt and recommended that she pay it off. Hopefully, she will listen to my advice and act on it as well.

All of those forms of debt add risk to your life. In the event you lose your ability to earn an income will determine if you will be able to repay the debt. What if you become disabled due to an injury, or you get a divorce and your spouse is the primary bread winner and he leaves you with all of the debt to repay (with you being a stay-at-home mom whom has not worked in several years)?

The reason that companies like my former debt buying employer and others exist is because people use debt. Some people were not able to repay the debt because of various reasons such as job loss, injury, disability, or may have been irresponsible and decided not to repay it. Whatever the situation, the debt was not repaid. People lose hope because they do not think that they can move forward financially due to the burden of debt. As a culture, Americans have been brainwashed to depend on debt. Here are some of the lies that we have been told so many years about debt that has made us rely on it.

What You May Have Heard: You need a credit card to pay for emergencies.

I spoke at one of my alma maters, and after the event my wife and I were going to eat dinner with the professor that invited me and his wife. The professor's wife stated that people need at least one credit card for emergencies. I did not respond because during my presentation I expressed my view point about credit cards. I had a credit card and used it for travel expenses, not emergencies. I probably would have used it for emergencies if needed. Many people may share the same sentiment as the professor's wife.

What You Need To Hear: You can use cash to pay for emergencies.

The real truth is that you do not need a credit card to pay for emergencies. Paying cash for emergencies is the best way to cover unexpected events. When you have money in the bank, your responses to unexpected events will be proactive, instead of reactive. Having a Rainy Day Fund gives you the security and peace of mind when life throws you a curve ball or puts a monkey wrench in your life. *Cash rules and debt is dumb.*

What You May Have Heard: Use other people's money to get what you want.

What a novel idea to borrow someone else's money to buy things that you want and pay it back later! Awesome! Imagine borrowing money at a low interest rate, say 3%, and pay it back at a later date. You make your purchase and repay the money and not pay a lot of money to get the item(s) that will enrich your lifestyle. Using "someone else's" money to pay for luxuries and even necessities is how the American culture has been taught to spend.

What You Need To Hear: You will be penalized for using someone else's money.

When you borrow money, whether at a high interest rate or a low interest rate, you will be penalized. How? Because when you pay interest for borrowing money you are paying a penalty. For example, if you get a $20,000 loan to buy a car (because you do not have the money to purchase it) at 5% interest for six years, you will have to repay $23,191. You will have paid a $3,191 penalty for borrowing $20,000. Borrowing other people's money will cost you more money than you originally borrowed.

What You May Have Heard: Buying a new car is the only way to get a reliable car.

Buying a brand-new car could possibly give you a more reliable car for many years in comparison to buying a used car. Finding a dependable used car can be difficult, so financing a new car could improve your chances of getting a car that will last you until the next time you are in the market for a new ride. In addition, having a new car could possibly increase your status among your peers and allow you to impress the people that have hated on you in the past, especially that bully back in your sixth-grade algebra class. Plus, you can afford the monthly car payment (that allows you to keep that new car smell!).

What You Need To Hear: You can buy a reliable used car without getting a car payment.

When you buy a new car from a dealership, as soon as you drive it off the lot the price of the car plummets like someone skydiving from an airplane! According to Edmunds.com, on average a new car loses 11% of its value the moment you leave the lot. After five years, the car is worth 37% of what you paid for it at the dealership![3] Imagine buying a $36,072 car, which is the average auto loan according to Experian.[4] The car would be worth $32,104 the moment you leave the dealership, and in five years the car would be worth $13,347! In addition, you would have to repay the car loan, pay for maintenance, car tags/taxes, and insurance. And there is a possibility that the car could have mechanical issues like a defective transmission or electrical problems causing it to not be as reliable as you thought.

However, you can find reliable, used cars for sale. When my Oldsmobile was stolen, I purchased a used 1996 Toyota Corolla. I bought it from an individual for $900 and had money remaining after the purchase to get auto insurance for it as well. Shameka and I had that car for four years. Today, we have two paid for cars (1996 Honda Civic and 1999 Honda Accord) that we paid for with cash. I have never had a car payment and do not plan to ever have one. I suggest paying cash for cars and staying free of car payments.

What You May Have Heard: Getting a payday loan will help me get ahead financially.

If you are struggling and living paycheck to paycheck, there are options available to you to help you get ahead until your next pay day. There are companies that offer payday loans, or cash advances, to you until you get paid again. For example, if you are short on cash and do not have the money to pay a utility bill, you can go to a payday loan company to get the money needed to help you with that cash shortage. Sound like a great idea?

What You Need To Hear: Payday loan companies are not in the business of helping you get ahead financially.
In fact, payday loans are a horrible financial instrument! According to the Federal Trade Commission, "Payday loans are small, short-term loans. They're usually for $500 or less, and typically have to be repaid within two to four weeks. Also called cash advance loans, they are legal in most states."[5] Here's how a payday loan works: You want to borrow a $100, so you write a $115 check, which includes a $15 fee. The company holds your check until your next pay day, and you either pay the $115, the company deposits the check, or you "roll" the amount into another loan (i.e., you borrow more money for an additional fee). You would have borrowed $100 at 15%. Borrowing money at 15% is not a smart money decision. The payday company wins, and you lose -- more money than you borrowed. My wife, Shameka, became prey to multiple payday loan companies, and she has decided never to borrow money from such companies again! I recommend staying far, far away from these loan sharks that are out to prey on the American consumer.

What You May Have Heard: I will borrow money from my 401(k) plan and repay it later. It's my money.
Borrowing money from your 401(k) plan, or retirement plan offered by your employer, is another option at your disposal for cash flow. You may decide to withdraw money from your 401(k) plan to go on a vacation, to upgrade your home with a new patio deck, or for a down payment on a new recreational vehicle. Your thought may be, "I have worked hard for this money, so I will withdraw some of it to enjoy life." You decide to withdraw $1,000 from your retirement plan. Then, after getting the money you say, "Was this a good decision? What is the worst that could happen?"

What You Need To Hear: Borrowing money from your 401(k) plan is not a wise financial decision.
When I worked as an auditor, one of my co-workers borrowed money from her 401(k) plan to repair the roof on her home. She was in the process of repaying the loan. By withdrawing money from your 401(k) plan you will be penalized. Here's how.

First, if you withdraw money before you are age 59 ½, you will pay a 10% penalty for early withdrawal. Second, if you leave your job, whether voluntarily or involuntarily, the loan will become due within 30-60 days. Third, not only will you pay a 10% penalty for early withdrawal, you will

18

also pay tax on the amount withdrawn at your normal tax rate; so if you are in a 15% tax bracket, you will pay 25% in taxes (10% penalty and 15% tax rate). Lastly, by borrowing from your 401(k) plan, you forgo the possibility of your money growing in the future. The money withdrawn has the potential to be worth more in the future than it is today.

What You May Have Heard: I will borrow money from a family member instead of a bank because I will not have to pay interest.

You and your brother, Larry, have a close relationship. You need some cash to help you with an unexpected event such as a major car repair. You ask Larry if you can borrow $2,000 from him to repair the car, and you promise to repay him when you get your income tax refund. When tax time comes, you get your tax refund and decide to wait until you get a bonus to repay Larry. You think, "Larry will understand. He knows that I am a dependable person that will repay him."

What You Need To Hear: Borrowing money from a family member will strain or destroy your relationship.

Larry will not understand why you have not repaid him. Borrowing money from a family member will either strain or destroy your relationship with that person(s). The relationship between you and Larry (from the example above) may become strained because you have now become the slave to Larry. If you go on vacation and still owe Larry money, he probably is going to wonder how you are able to spend money for a vacation while owing him money. Or, what if you lose your job and cannot repay the money? More than likely you and Larry's relationship may deteriorate until the money is repaid in full.

I let my parents borrow money for a vehicle repair and to purchase a used vehicle. My mother's van needed repairing, while my dad desperately needed another car because his transmission stopped working on his Lincoln Continental. I loaned my parents about $2,900. They began repaying the money; however, the dynamic of the relationship shifted from them being my parents and me being their son to them being my slave and me being their master. Scripture says, "Just as the rich rule the poor, so the borrower is servant to the lender."[6] This Scripture describes what my relationship had become. So how did I resolve the lender/slave relationship with my parents? I forgave the debt and told them that the money was a gift.

What You May Have Heard: Co-signing allows me to help my friend or family member get a loan.

What is co-signing? Co-signing is when one person agrees to be responsible for someone else's loan. For example, if I want to buy a motorcycle but do not have a good credit score to show that I have repaid money that I have borrowed. I ask my mother (whom in this example has a good credit score) to sign for the loan on my behalf while I repay the loan. That means that my mother is responsible for making the car payment if I refuse or cannot repay the loan. Is this a win-win situation?

What You Need To Hear: Co-signing for someone else's loan is a really bad idea.

By getting a co-signer, the lender knows that the person being co-signed for is not likely to repay the loan. Therefore, the co-signer will be liable for the loan and have to pay it back to the lender. The co-signer ultimately loses in this deal, and the lender is the victor. The Bible says, "Don't agree to guarantee another person's debt or put up security for someone else. If you can't pay it, even your bed will be snatched from under you."[7] Take heed and refuse to co-sign a loan for anyone.

Many years ago, a cousin of mine asked me to co-sign for a jeep for him. To my knowledge, he is the only person that has ever asked me to co-sign for a loan. I told my cousin that I would not co-sign for him. Later, that same cousin got into trouble and went to jail. Had I co-signed, I would have been stuck with repaying the loan. If someone asks you to co-sign for a loan, immediately say no. Because if you agree, you will eventually pay for the loan, whether you want to or not.

What You May Have Heard: I can get a home equity line of credit to take a vacation or to pay for a home improvement.

A home equity line of credit, or HELOC, is when someone borrows money on their home. The person has equity in his home and wants to withdraw the equity from the home to make purchases. A HELOC is also known as a second mortgage because you are borrowing additional money on your home. Getting a second mortgage is available for you to acquire money for purchases. The process is just like getting a first mortgage because you go through the same process as you did when obtaining your primary mortgage. People may get a HELOC to pay for vacation, college education, or to do a home improvement project.

What You Need To Hear: A HELOC adds more risk to your life.

Borrowing money against your home is not a wise idea. Here's why. When you get a HELOC, you are borrowing money at a higher interest rate because if you are not able to pay your first mortgage payment, more than likely you will not be able to pay the second mortgage either. So the lender for the second mortgage will likely not get paid; that is the reason you are charged a higher interest rate because if you cannot make your mortgage payments, the lender on the first mortgage has precedence in receiving any proceeds from the sale of your house once it is in foreclosure. In addition, you are adding more risk to your life by borrowing money against your house. You put your family's livelihood in jeopardy by getting a HELOC. You could lose your home. Say "yes" to a first mortgage, but "no" to a second mortgage.

What You May Have Heard: Debt is a tool that I can use to prosper.

Some people may see debt as a tool to use to prosper financially. Debt may be used to start a business, buy a car, further one's education, buy a house, and for other uses. Debt is available to people to help them make purchases instantaneously. Use credit, or debt, now and repay later. If you need inventory or equipment to start your business, debt may allow you to get the items needed for start-up. Or, if you want to get an education to improve your career opportunities, getting a student loan will help you move in the right direction. Debt is an option.

What You Need To Hear: Debt is not a tool. It is a thief that steals.

The truth about debt is that it is not a tool. It is a thief that is stealing your dreams and hopes. When you have payments such as car payments, student loan payments, credit card payments, and mortgage payments, you are in bondage until you set yourself free. Being in debt means that you are enslaved to the whims of the lender. When you have debt, the money that you spend "enjoying" like going on a summer vacation is not your money because you owe someone (a lender) money. Having debt payments robs you of saving for unexpected events, retirement, giving, and wealth accumulation. And, ultimately, it is stealing your future dreams.

What if you did not have any debt? What if you did not owe anyone a single penny? What could you do for your family? What could you do for your local community? What could you do for your global community? The possibilities are endless! When you borrow money, you are a servant as the Proverb states: "Just as the rich rule the poor, so the borrower is servant to the lender."[8]

God wants us to live debt free. He wants us to live a life free of financial debt. When you have debt, you add risk and stress to your life. When you are debt free, you have options.

How to Stop the Dream Killer

The idea of living debt free is counter-intuitive and goes against the culture in North America. We live in a culture that tells us that we need things now. Instead of saving money to make purchases, we decide to borrow money at high interest rates, large payments, and lengthy loan terms. To see that a debt free lifestyle is the ideal way to live, I must convince you that it is worthwhile. In order for you to understand this idea, you must change your perspective about debt. First, you must have a "Why" for living debt free. Why do you want to live debt free? Is the reason because you want to reduce the risk in your personal life? Or, is it because you want to retire with dignity and not depend on the U.S. Federal government to meet your financial needs? You must decide your "Why." My "Why" is threefold: 1) I grew up living on welfare and do not want to live like that again (EVER!); 2) I want to provide for my beautiful wife the best I can offer; and 3) I want to give my daughter the best life can offer and leave a legacy for her and my grandchildren.

Next, you must decide not to ever borrow money again, with the exception of a home loan (i.e., fifteen year fixed-rate mortgage). That means, no car loans, credit cards, student loans, or payday loans ever again! You must decide from this point forward to never borrow money. This is where you draw a line in the sand (figuratively speaking), and choose to do something different; something that WILL change your life and your family!

Once you know your reason for getting out of debt (i.e., your "Why") and decide to live debt free, you must earn extra income to put toward your debt. How can you earn extra income? You could work overtime (O.T.) at work. If your employer allows you to put in some O.T., get as much overtime as you can. Another option is to get a part-time job. You could work at a restaurant, retail store, or anywhere that needs additional help providing a product or service. Or, maybe you could start a small business to increase your income. You may have a skill or talent that you could use to add value to people's lives and earn a little (or a lot) of money to accelerate your debt elimination plan. Whether you owe $1,000, $10,000, or $100,000, you can pay off your debt.

Debt Crusher Method

Now that you have all the ingredients to get out of debt, here is the process to destroy the dream killer. The process is called the Debt Crusher Method. With the Debt Crusher Method, you list your debts tiniest to biggest regardless of the interest rate. Pay the minimum required monthly payment on each debt. Pay as much as you can on the tiniest debt by earning more income to crush it quickly! Then, apply the amount you were paying on the first debt to the second debt to crush it. The minimum payment you paid on the first debt will be added to the minimum payment of the second debt (and any extra money you can pay). Continue this process for each debt. As you pay off each debt on your list, you will have more money to pay on the next debt. Keep crushing debt until you have completely destroyed your debt to become debt free!

Becoming debt free is hard work, but it is worth the effort. In order to become debt free, you must be FOCUSED, FIERCE, and ON FIRE! This process will not happen without the elements mentioned earlier in this chapter combined with focus, fierceness, and being on fire (i.e., passion mixed with action) about crushing debt to reclaim your dream. You can become debt free if you decide. I have already decided. Now it is your turn.

Action Steps to Maximize Your Money to Stop Being Broke

1. Make a conscious decision to stop borrowing money and to never borrow it again, with the exception of a home mortgage (see guidelines discussed earlier in the chapter).
2. Request a copy of your credit report from the three credit bureaus (Equifax, Experian, and TransUnion). You should be able to request a free credit report once a year from each credit bureau. Search online for information about free annual credit reports. Then, make a list of all of your debts using the information from your credit reports and any other debts that you have.
3. List your debts from tiniest to biggest using the Debt Crusher Method form in the Broke Management Forms section near the end of the book. Start crushing your debt!

4
Savvy Saving
Beefing Up the Rainy Day Fund

Imagine if you were working for a company for ten years, and one day your supervisor called you into her office. She said, "Angela, I have to let you know that today is your last day with the company. We had to eliminate your position. The company needed to reduce some expenses, and your position got selected to be dissolved. However, you will get two month's severance pay for your service." How would you feel? Defeated? Shocked? Well, you knew that your employer struggled to make a profit the last three years. Even though you saw the signs of the company's decline, you failed to prepare for the unexpected (even though the signs were very, very clear). The company will provide a nice severance package when you depart from its premises. However, a two month severance can only keep you afloat for a short period of time. You did not save for this event; you had no Rainy Day Fund ready for the job loss. Not being prepared leads to stress, fear, and anxiety. This is one scenario. Let's look at an alternative situation.

The facts of this scenario are the same as mentioned above, but what if you had $10,000 in your Rainy Day Fund for unexpected events. How would you feel? Better than previously described. There would be some fear of the unknown because you have devoted ten years of your life to this company and starting over again is scary, but is also full of new possibilities! What if you got another job within one month? Instead of using the severance to pay for monthly expenses, you could put that money toward other financial goals! In the second scenario, you were ready with not only a $1,500 Rainy Day Fund you had $10,000 saved for life's BIG unexpected events! The second scenario is the life of someone that plans and is on a mission to keep crises from occurring in her life.

Now that you know the "Why" of having a Rainy Day Fund, in this chapter we will elaborate on the concept of saving for unexpected events.

The $10K+ Marathon
Saving money is a habit that many people do not possess. In fact, saving money must become a habit if you want to accumulate wealth. Becoming a savvy saver is a discipline that takes time. Going from a consumption mentality to one of a savvy saver requires a new way of thinking and a new perspective. Saving must be a priority and important to you. In order to increase your $1,500 Rainy Day Fund to $10,000 or more takes

discipline and the willingness to sacrifice in the short term to get long term results. Why do you want to have $10,000 (or more) in a Rainy Day Fund? Well, personally, my wife and I have realized that when you have money set aside for unexpected events, when those events happen you are ready to attack them proactively instead of reactively. That means, when your washing machine stops working, you have the money to fix the problem and not let it derail your financial plan. Or, if your spouse gets laid off from work, you all can stay afloat until he finds another job.

In addition, another benefit of having a mega Rainy Day Fund is that unexpected events are far and in between; they do not happen that often. It is as if life knows to bypass you when it comes to disasters. But, if you do not have a Rainy Day Fund, life throws you as many curve balls as possible to get you off course.

What's the Magic Number?

So how much money should you put in your mega Rainy Day Fund? I recommend having three to nine months of living expenses saved in your Rainy Day Fund (after you become debt free). Depending on how much you spend on your primary necessities (i.e., food, shelter/utilities, transportation, and basic clothing), three to nine months of living expenses could range between $10,000 and $30,000 in savings. If your air conditioning and heating unit stops working in the summer time, you will be prepared to pay $5,000 to replace the unit. Or, what if your clothes dryer needs repairing or replacing in the winter time? You have the $4,500 to repair or replace the clothes dryer. No debt required; just cash in the bank. It's that simple. You will have planned to curb those unexpected events, so that you can keep moving forward, instead of backward. Those are just some examples of how having a mega Rainy Day Fund can help you stay on track toward your financial goals. Once you have paid for the major unexpected event, replenish your account back to the three to nine months amount.

By having $10,000 in your bank account, you will become a "thousandnaire." What is a thousandnaire you might ask? A thousandnaire is when someone saves thousands of dollars before saving millions of dollars to become a millionaire. However, your three to nine months of living expenses is not for purchases.

You Mean I Can Spend This Money? Yes! But...

Again, the whole purpose of having a supersized, savings account, or the three to nine months of living expenses in a Rainy Day Fund, is to protect you from life's major unexpected events. The Rainy Day Fund will be your life preserver to save you from going back into debt to pay for the roof on your house when it starts to leak during a thunderstorm. In essence, your mega Rainy Day Fund is like insurance to protect you from life's unexpected happenings.

You Mean I Can't Go On A Spending Spree?!

Some people may think that having a large sum of cash in the bank is great! It is, however, your mega Rainy Day Fund is not for making purchases. The Rainy Day Fund is not for buying a new living room set, a big screen television to watch the national championship football game, or a new luxury car with all of latest bells and whistles.

Some people may be tempted to use the money for investing to accumulate wealth. Building wealth is one of the goals to obtain, but at this stage of the process using the Rainy Day Fund for wealth building is premature. Why? Because you need the Rainy Day Fund as a foundational element in your financial plan that will help propel you to accumulate wealth. If you decide to invest the $10,000 sitting in your Rainy Day Fund in a mutual fund (we will discuss this concept later), you will leave nothing in the account. Well, as soon as you withdraw the money from the bank account and put it into the mutual fund, your engine will stop working on your car; or, your refrigerator in your home will need replacing. Anything that can happen will likely happen when you use the Rainy Day Fund for investing.

According to Bankrate, 39% of Americans could comfortably cover an unexpected expense of $1,000.[1] I do not want you to become part of this statistic of people that are not prepared. Be ready for the rain!

Where Should the Rainy Day Fund Be?

When you start saving for your Rainy Day Fund, I suggest putting the money in a regular savings account at your local bank or credit union. Be sure that you can access your money by writing a check or withdrawal via an automated teller machine (ATM).

I would not suggest keeping your Rainy Day Fund in your sock drawer or under your bed. Having it in those places gives you access to the money, but such convenience ushers in the temptation to use the money for things other than unexpected events.

What are the Benefits of the Mega Rainy Day Fund?

What's in it for you? Having three to nine months of living expenses in your Rainy Day Fund will:

- *Help you move toward not being broke by keeping unexpected events from ruining your financial plan.*
- *Keep you emotionally sane and far away from living in crisis mode.*
- *Remove the stress, worry, and fear that may lead to physical ailments.*

- *Reduce the money fights with your spouse (if you are married).*
- *Give you an option to combat the urges to use debt.*
- *Allow you to continue to focus on the important people and things in your life.*

I hope you are convinced that having a mega Rainy Day Fund will benefit you, your family, and give you the peace of mind to continue your journey to maximize your money and stop being broke. I encourage you to become a savvy saver from this day forward because saving money is important. Once you establish a discipline of saving, then you will have the tools necessary for the next phase to level up your finances: Wealth Accumulation. But for now, let's discuss making wise purchases.

Action Steps to Maximize Your Money to Stop Being Broke
1. Understand the importance of saving money.
2. Decide to make saving important and a priority in your life. Make it a habit.
3. Decide how much is three to nine months of living expenses for you, and increase your mini Rainy Day Fund to a mega amount.

Purposeful Purchases
Intentional Spending Habits

As a small business owner, sometimes I think about the many different businesses when I drive. Once, my wife and I were going to lead a personal finance class in Madison, Tennessee, a suburb of Nashville. I thought to myself, "People are in business; whether they selling products and services that help or hurt people, companies are open for business." Most of the businesses are small businesses. As I drove down the street through the various traffic lights, I could not help but notice all of the billboards and signs of the different entities: restaurants, a bank, credit unions, and shopping mall. All of them had one thing in common: They were trying to advertise their product or service.

In the marketplace, this is called marketing. Marketing is simply when companies use different ways to get their products and services to customers. Business owners and managers of companies know, (or should know) that every person in the world is not going to buy their product. They have to make sure that their efforts and money are targeting the right people. Marketers spend billions of dollars on television and Internet marketing. That means that companies are spending a lot of money to get your business and your money!

Marketing 101 from College
When I pursued my first bachelor's degree at a Kentucky college I majored in marketing. My professor, Martie Kazura, taught two marketing classes that I really liked entitled, Consumer Behavior and Marketing Research. I do not remember every aspect that Martie taught, but here is a variation of it. In my marketing class, we discussed the four "Ps", which stand for product, price, position, and place. The first, P is obvious; companies have a product (or service) of value to sell to customers that meets a need or want. A pair of shoes, for example, is a valuable product to customers if they do not like walking on concrete or grass with bare feet. The second P stands for price. The product must be reasonably priced in comparison to similar products that satisfy a need. Those tennis shoes should be reasonably priced whether you buy them from a large department store or purchase them online.

The third P represents the position, or how consumers view a certain product versus another. For example, people may think that a pair of Nike Air Jordan's is superior to a pair of Reebok Shaquille O'Neal's;

both of those athletes are hall of famers, but the consumer's perception determines who has the better shoe. Companies help mold the consumers' perception through marketing. Lastly, the fourth P stands for place, or distribution. In other words, place is how companies get their products to customers or to a physical location. The retail shoe store that sells shoes orders hundreds of pairs of shoes from the shoe manufacturer to sell to customers. The shoes would probably be shipped, or distributed, from the manufacturer to the retail store via tracker trailer truck.

I told you about my marketing background because I want you to know one thing about companies: They have a plan. That plan includes getting your money. It's not bad that businesses want to meet your wants and needs in exchange for money, but I want you to have a plan for your money as well, so that you do not give all of it away! Businesses spend a whole lot of money to convince you to buy their products and services. Beware of the tactics that are used to market to you and persuade you to make unplanned purchases.

Marketing Tactics to Get Your Money

People are in business to make money by serving you to meet a desired need or want. If businesses do not earn your money by selling products or services, those businesses disappear; they close their doors. That is the reason that businesses spend billions of dollars on marketing to attract your attention in hopes that you will buy. Every day we are bombarded with hundreds of marketing messages on billboards, social media, e-mail, radio, TV, and magazines. Our job is to become informed consumers. I do not want you to be paranoid about the buying process. I want you to be knowledgeable and wise. Here are some of the mediums that companies use to get your dollars.

Social Media

With the advent of the social media platforms such as Facebook, Twitter, Instagram, and others, businesses are using social media to get their message to the desired customers. When I am logged into my Facebook account or Twitter account, I see ads promoting products and services of different companies. Obviously, not everyone uses social media. However, I mentioned earlier that companies spend billions of dollars on Internet marketing. As you scroll through the feeds on your social media pages, be aware of the marketing that is happening. Be aware so that you do not unexpectedly click on an ad and make a purchase that you did not plan.

Traditional Avenues: TV, Radio, and Print
Television (TV)
Alright, who grew up in a family that had two TVs in the living room? One TV was broken and the other one worked; usually the broken one was the larger TV and the functioning TV, usually a smaller TV, was on top of the broken one. I wondered why people kept the broken TV. I guess they were afraid that the little TV would get lonely.

Even though TV has been around for decades, it is still considered an effective mass-marketing format. TV advertising is so effective because of repetition, and TV remains the best advertising for cashed-up marketers who are willing to spend large amounts on ad campaigns for mass audiences.[1] Companies know the power of repetition and use it well with TV. Whether you are watching your favorite sitcom, sporting event, romance movie, or action series, TV ads will be present to entice you to make a future purchase.

Radio
Another medium that companies use is radio advertising. As you listen to your favorite tunes on the radio, between songs are commercials advertising to you to get your dollars. In fact, radio stations sell advertising space to businesses and those businesses' products and services are broadcast over the airwaves. According to Nielsen, during first quarter 2020, 91% of adults listened to the radio each week, more than any other medium.[2] Internet radio and podcasting have exploded with companies such as Pandora and Anchor, which allow people to listen to their favorite music online or on their smartphones and create content via podcasts. While streaming your music online or listening to a podcast, you may hear advertisements. Although the radio personality or announcer says, "Sorry to interrupt your music...," the companies that bought the advertising space is not apologetic. The advertisement is intentional. Remember: The companies have a plan, so be aware.

Print
I like to read a good old fashioned, hardcopy book. Don't you? Well, print such as magazines and newspapers is another way businesses market their products and services to you. When I was an auditor, I would read some of the airline magazines during the plane flight. I remember one particular magazine that had a famous actor showcasing a specific watch. The advertisement was clearly marketing to high-net worth individuals. Although the publishing industry has changed with the popularity of the Internet, print advertising still has a place for advertising. Some people, including me, like to read a hardcopy of books and magazines, and marketers know this about their desired target audience. Despite being in

the Digital Age, print advertising is just an additional avenue for businesses to get their message out into the marketplace.

Have It Your Way: Now, Not Later

We live in a microwave society, meaning we want things now! We cannot wait to save money to make a purchase, so we go into debt to get the latest gadget, vehicle, or house when we really need to wait. Companies are making purchasing their products easier than ever before with convenience methods such as PayPal and Square. Those convenience methods allow customers to use their debit or credit cards to buy items normally offered only by stores that had credit card machines. Now, consumers can swipe their cards while attending a conference to buy a recommended book, a t-shirt at a music concert, or to pay for a drink at a basketball game. In fact, I have a PayPal card reader that I use at my financial workshops to accept debit card payments for participant admission. With convenient payment methods, the temptation to make an impulse purchase increases.[3]

Another convenience method that companies use is the "90 Days Same as Cash" tactic. With this tactic, companies offer consumers products with no interest payments for ninety days. The consumer can pay off the item within ninety days and pay no interest. However, if the item, say a washing machine, is not paid in full within the ninety days, the consumer will have to pay the interest that has accrued, or accumulated. You would pay the cost of the original item plus the unpaid interest. More than likely, the company would not have explained to the customer how the 90 Days Same as Cash method works, which means the customer would be caught off-guard and probably upset. This is the reason why I want you to have a plan for your money and be an informed consumer. Ninety days is not the same as cash. Cash rules!

Other Marketing Tactics to Get Your Cash

Thus far we have discussed several ways companies market to you to get their hands in your pocket. I am a consumer as well, so I am not exempt from the marketing methods outlined in this chapter. I must be on guard as well because I can become a victim to unplanned purchases, too. Here are several more ways businesses try to persuade you to give them your money.

Shelf Space

From time to time, Shameka and I will go grocery shopping together. Now, you are probably thinking, "I hate to go shopping!" Well, as a guy, personally I like to shop and accompany my wife as well. We make a grocery list, so that we do not impulse shop and to stay within our budget.

Shameka will normally have the list gathering items from the shelves, while I push Naomi in her stroller or the shopping cart. Sometimes when getting groceries, Shameka will ask me to help her get an item from a top shelf. I am a little taller than six feet, which helps in situations like this. Well, companies consider height when it comes to selling their goods.

In particular, grocery stores, strategically position their products on shelves in a certain way to make it convenient for you to buy them. They use the shelf space to place higher priced, more desirable items at "eye level" and lower priced items on the higher and lower shelves. More than likely, the name brand items will be placed at eye level, or where you can easily see and purchase them. And, the makers of those items probably paid a premium to place their goods at eye level.

Another shelf space tactic that is used is the point of sale. Point of sale items are placed near the cash register such as chewing gum, sodas, beef jerky, and candy. Those items are placed specifically for impulse shopping. Think about it: You are waiting in line to check out your groceries, and you have to wait ten minutes. While you are waiting your child asks for some chocolate candy from the point-of-sale area. To calm her, you get the candy and put it in your cart. Then, you see a soda in a small freezer in the same area; you open the freezer to get an ice cold drink and add it to your cart. Without thinking, you have added two items that you did not plan because the store had a plan, but you were not paying attention and fell for the trap.

The next time you go grocery shopping, pay attention to the shelf position of the items in the store and to the point-of-sale area.

Color

Have you ever driven past a bright red car and tried to avoid looking at it? Or, how about a bright green or yellow vehicle? Our eyes are attracted to vibrant, bright colors such as red, orange, and yellow. Marketers know that colors draw our attention, and they use this in their marketing strategies to get you to look at their goods and make a purchasing decision. For example, Shameka and I buy a certain manufacturer's toothpaste, and one time I noticed the color of the packaging was bright red with yellow and gold-like colors. The colors alone drew my attention to look at the box.

Packaging

Companies also use packaging as a means to market to you. Some products are packaged in a way that appeal to our senses and entice us to want to make a purchase. Businesses pay special attention to create a package that fits comfortably in the customer's hand. An item may be packaged specifically with clear packaging to show the features that would be otherwise hidden until the item is opened.

Brand Recognition

As a consumer, I am loyal to certain product brands. When it comes to toothpaste, facial soap, hand soap, and cars, I am a loyalist. That means I only will buy a certain brand of products. Brand recognition is your perception of a company or its products and services. That company helped you create a perspective of its products or services through marketing efforts to distinguish itself from the competitors. An example is a PC, or personal computer such as Microsoft, versus the Apple computer brand. A PC may have features and functions that the Apple computer does not have, or vice versa. By you and me being loyal to a brand, the company's product that we perceive as superior to the competition, is a result of marketing efforts to get us to make purchases, planned or unplanned.

The marketing strategies discussed in this chapter are tools to help you become a wise and informed consumer. I want you to shop with confidence knowing that you are armed with knowledge to guard against the many marketing tactics that are hurled at us every day. Before we talk about the plan to keep your money, let's address a guideline for major purchases.

Is It A Major or Minor League Purchase?

When I bought my first car in high school, it felt really, really good! To be sixteen years old and buying my first car was a big accomplishment. Even at that age I paid cash for the car. I worked hard to save money for my 1986 Oldsmobile Cutlass Supreme; I sacrificed by not buying a lot of clothes to get my car. I was determined to save the money regardless of the naysayers. My parents were generous enough to add me to their car insurance policy, and I paid my portion of the bill, which helped me become more responsible and have a low insurance payment. I paid $900 for the car. At that time, I did not have the knowledge that I have now, but I knew that that was a lot of money for someone my age! In my opinion, that car purchase was a major one for two reasons. First, I earned the money to buy a car as a teenager and achieved a personal goal I had set. Second, it was a major purchase because of the dollar amount spent.

What is a major purchase? Dave Ramsey defines a major purchase as any amount that is $300 or more. I am going to build on his guideline and define a major purchase as any amount that is $200 or more. That means my car purchase was a major purchase. These definitions of a major purchase are guidelines because people have different income levels. If your annual income is $35,000, then $200 may be a significant purchase in your world. But if your annual income is $350,000 a $200 purchase would be a blip on your financial radar (unless you are living paycheck to paycheck, which I hope you are not). The $200 is a boundary for making major purchases, so that you do not experience regret. I will explain more about this later in the chapter.

Making a big purchase can be exciting! In fact, research shows that the act of purchasing is like being on drugs because a hormone called dopamine, which flows into your brain, activates the pleasure centers of our brain causing us to get excited.[4] So buying causes our bodies to change physically and mentally, and many of us may not know about these affects. That is probably the reason why some people become addicted to shopping because of the "high" caused by the hormones. In making a major purchase, you will experience this "high" and feeling of excitement, so be careful when making big purchases.

Another emotion that people may feel when they have made a big purchase decision is buyer's remorse. Buyer's remorse is when people experience the pleasure of buying and later encounter an overwhelming feeling of regret. An example may be when Joey buys a new $40,000 car. Day one of driving the car he is filled with joy and happiness, and day two Joey is flooded with feelings of regret for buying the car; he realizes that the purchase was a mistake and tries to return it to the dealership. He is disappointed that the dealership will not accept the car without payment in full. Ouch! I do not want what happened to Joey to happen to you. Now that we have discussed what a major purchase is, let's look at some ways to spend on purpose.

Purposeful Purchases: Spending with a Plan

I want you to know that you are not alone in this process. Let me assure you that I have made stupid purchasing mistakes just like you. I have learned from them and hope you have as well. Let me reiterate: Companies have a plan to get your money. You must have a plan to keep your money; it is fine to buys things, but I want you to spend wisely. Let's discuss how to make wise purchase decisions.

Getting Control When Making Purchases

I know what I am going to say should be obvious, but I am going to say it. You must live within your means to get control of your spending habits. Gaining control starts and ends with you. You must live on your Monthly Money Plan. Living on a monthly budget, giving, saving, investing, and spending wisely is the only way to live; period. Now, let's get a game plan for making major purchases.

Wise Ways for Making Major Purchases:
Put Off Purchasing for 24 – 48 Hours

First, before making a major purchase I recommend putting off your purchase for 24 – 48 hours. Why? I suggest waiting because of the emotional feelings that surface when getting ready to buy. Remember the pleasure centers in the brain are being activated by the act, not possession, of a purchase. By waiting you allow those feelings to decrease, allowing you to think more clearly without the influence of pleasure inducing hormones. In addition, you avoid the emotional crash of regret that follows the climatic high.

Determine If the Purchase Is a Want or Need

In America, it's easy to get a want and a need confused. Let's define the two. A need is basic food, shelter, and clothing. Those are needs; we need food and water to live. We need shelter to protect us from the weather and other outdoor elements. And, we need clothes to wear, so that we do not go to jail for indecent exposure. Just joking! We could discuss other things like the Internet, air conditioning, and cell phones and attempt to categorize them into the want and need boxes, but that would be difficult because everyone has a different perspective on wants and needs.

A want is anything that is beyond the basic necessities that we need to live. Let me give some examples. If I had one pair of shoes, my need for shoes would be met; however, if I have five pairs of shoes, the additional four pairs are wants. A phone is necessary for communication; we need to communicate with people. I could easily write letters to my parents in South Carolina, which would be sufficient, but not efficient. In this day and age, having a phone is considered a necessity and getting a smartphone is definitely a want.

So before making a major purchase, determine if the item is a want or a need. Ask yourself, "Do I need this item or just want it?" Scripture says, "Don't be concerned about the outward beauty of fancy hairstyles, expensive jewelry, or beautiful clothes. You should clothe yourselves instead with the beauty that comes from within, the unfading beauty of a gentle and quiet spirit, which is precious to God."[5]

Be Content

Before making a major purchase decision, check yourself by asking, "Am I happy without this purchase? Am I content before I spend this money?" Contentment is an important concept in this journey to not being broke. Money can buy material things and fun, but not happiness. Stephen Covey, author of the *7 Habits of Highly Effective People*, said "We are responsible for our own effectiveness, for our own happiness, and ultimately, [...] for most of our circumstances."[6] In addition, Scripture states, "So if we have enough food and clothing, let us be content."[7]

First, Understand; Then, Buy

I have experienced making dumb purchases because I simply did not understand what I was buying. I bought a "lemon" car from an auction because I did not understand that it was rigged only to be sold to an uninformed consumer like me. I bought a mattress without the bed frame because I did not fully read the invoice. Both the buyer and seller have a responsibility in the purchasing process, but ultimately it is the buyer's responsibility to first understand the product or service she is buying. Then, after understanding, make an informed purchase.

Can You Spend the Money Elsewhere?

There are always alternative things you could buy instead of your original purchase. Before making a significant purchasing decision, ask yourself, "Can I spend this money on something else?" For instance, Trinity wants to spend $4,500 to go on a cruise to Saint Lucia, a country in the Caribbean. Trinity also wants to pay on her credit card debt. She can only do one of the two options, but not both. If she goes to Saint Lucia, she will have fun with her friends and create memories for a life time. On the other hand, Trinity will still have credit card debt when she returns home from Saint Lucia. There is always a tradeoff when making a major purchase. You have to choose the best option for your situation.

Consult with Your Spouse or Accountability Partner

Shameka and I are best friends. I can confide in her because she knows me and understands me (for the most part!). We have a great relationship, and we talk often, which helps us have a healthy marriage. We especially consult each other when making major purchases. If you are married, I encourage you to do the same. By consulting with your spouse, you involve him in the process, get his perspective, and are able to hopefully agree on the purchase. Being in agreement with your spouse will let him know that you value his opinion and will make the relationship stronger. An old Proverb says, "Plans go wrong for lack of advice; many advisors bring success."[8]

If you are single, I recommend consulting with your accountability partner before making a big purchase decision. By doing so, you will avoid the feelings of regret, shame, and entitlement. Don't have an accountability partner? I recommend finding someone as soon as you finish reading this sentence. "Get all the advice and instruction you can, so you will be wise the rest of your life."[9]

Be On Guard

Lastly, I want you to always be on guard when making a significant purchase. Revisit this chapter often when making large purchases to refresh your memory, so that you will not fall prey to the marketing tactics of companies. It is fine to make purchases as long as your decisions are wise. Now that you have a game plan to make better buying decisions, let's discuss some ways to save even more money by negotiating.

Practical Negotiating Techniques

I remember going to the jockey lot or flee market when I was younger. I really enjoyed going to "window shop" because I liked seeing all of the items for sale. I am a cheapskate, so often I did not buy anything. You can probably find every item imaginable at a jockey lot for lower than market prices. That's one of the perks of going to a jockey lot. Another benefit is being able to negotiate even lower prices for products for sale. In fact, my brother Jeff is a master haggler, I mean, negotiator. Jeff can negotiate very well, especially when he wants to buy a car.

When my Oldsmobile was stolen, Jeff went with me to buy another car. At the time, the owner of the car was related to a friend of my brother Acea. Jeff and I went to the lady's house to see the car, and we test drove it. After driving the car, Jeff jumped into action to negotiate a better price for the car. He mentioned some of the problems with the car and asked for a lower price. After many hours of negotiating, I was able to buy the car for $900 cash and even had money left over to get car insurance! That's the power of negotiating! Bodean's, as we call Jeff, gift of price negotiating saved me money on the major purchase. Here are some practical negotiating techniques that you can use to become a better negotiator like Jeff.

Always Be Honest

This principle is applicable whether you are the buyer or the seller. Always be honest with people. I have had two cars that the transmissions stopped working. When I sold each car, I was honest with the customers because I want to treat people like I want to be treated. If you are not honest, the truth will eventually surface and the customer will tell his friends about your dishonesty, and you could possibly lose perspective customers. Whether you are selling clothes, jewelry, fruit, or hair spray, always be honest. Just follow Scripture's advice: "Do to others as you would like them to do to you."[10]

Flash Some Cash

Another negotiating technique that is sure to bring positive results (and a lower price!) is to flash some cash in front of the seller. Money talks! I have experienced the power of this technique. When I was trying to replace my Oldsmobile that was stolen, I took cold, hard cash with me to be my friend in the negotiating process. In addition to Jeff working his negotiating magic, the cash spoke a language of its own and allowed us to close the deal. If you are able (and not afraid to carry a lot of cash), I recommend taking some Uncle Benjamin Franklins (i.e., $100 dollar bills) with you as you negotiate on major purchases.

Be Able to Say "No" to the Deal

Imagine you are at the furniture store looking for a couch for your living room. As you browse the showroom, your eye is captured by a brown leather couch with a matching love seat. At that moment, you are flooded with feelings of excitement because you are about to buy this furniture set! However, the salesperson is not willing to negotiate the price. You were honest and flashed cash is her face to get a lower price, but she would not budge. Well, sometimes you will have to say "No" to a deal. Do not become attached to the item before negotiations have ended because you may not be able to close the deal and make the purchase, which will leave you upset and disappointed. Be able to walk away from the deal without becoming emotionally attached to the item.

Learn to Be Quiet

For an extrovert, learning to be quiet during a negotiation can be challenging. However, if we want to get the product at a desired price, being quiet must be a skill that we need to learn. Silence can feel uncomfortable. Have you ever been on a date with someone and did not know what to say? The moment of silence felt so awkward, right? Well, when negotiating for a better price silence is golden. Let me demonstrate. The seller tells you about the benefits of the product to educate you, gives you facts about the competitor's product, and then you offer a suggested purchase price. Afterward, be quiet. The quietness will feel very uncomfortable, but let its power work to get the seller to accept your price. Learning this technique can really help improve your negotiation skills.

Think Win-Win

During the negotiation process, both parties should benefit. There should be no win-lose or lose-win situations. Both the buyer and seller need to win. You want to buy a product at a reasonable price, and the seller wants to give you the item at a price that is profitable for him. If this scenario is not possible through negotiating, then as Stephen Covey says in the book *The 7 Habits of Highly Effective People*, "[There is a] higher expression of

Win/Win—Win/Win or No Deal."[11] Sometimes you may have to leave the negotiation empty handed.

Wisdom from the Trenches

As you apply these principles to your life you will become a wiser spender, especially when making significant purchases. Your buying decisions should improve over time because you are financially literate and have a plan to guard against the marketing tactics of businesses. I have learned from my mistakes and want to share my knowledge to help you make better and more informed buying choices and hopefully allow you to create great purchasing habits. Be intentional about keeping more of your money and giving less of it to companies that want to take it out of your pocket and bank account.

Bonus Lesson: Couponing

Before I end this chapter, I am compelled to add some more value to your life. Another way to save money is by using coupons. Shameka did couponing a couple of years ago for our family, and we saved a lot of money on our grocery bill! We had a stocked pantry full of food that lasted us for about a month. She went to various stores to get specials on a variety of food and toiletry items. We did not have to go to the grocery store that often.

In addition, Shameka would meet with a group of ladies from our church to clip, exchange, and organize coupons. She kept the coupons in a green binder, and they were categorized in a systematic manner. The group gave her a chance to establish a community with other like-minded women and allowed her to lower our grocery bill.

Although couponing is beneficial, it is also hard work. Gathering, clipping, and organizing coupons is challenging. And, if you add finding newspaper ads that supply the coupons to the already difficult task of couponing, this process is not for the faint at heart. If you decide that you want to try couponing, I recommend committing to the process for ninety days. I also recommend finding a group similar to the one Shameka attended to help you learn how to coupon and to give you support during the process.

Action Steps to Maximize Your Money to Stop Being Broke

1. Pre-decide with your spouse or accountability partner before making a major purchase that you will follow the guidelines discussed in this chapter.
2. Review this chapter every six months to stay aware of the marketing tactics used by companies.
3. Use the negotiation tips discussed when making major purchases.

Part II
Wealth Accumulation
6
Multi-Tasking for a Prosperous Future
Retirement, College Savings, and Mortgage Crushing
Task 1: Retirement

Let me check in with you. How has the adventure been so far? Enjoyable? Challenging? Fun? Scary? I am sure that you have felt all of these emotions so far on this journey to maximize your money to stop being broke. This process is not for the weak. After going through the process, you may feel weak from the effort that is needed to make changes in your life. But moving through the steps requires an immense amount of focus, fierceness, passion, and action to take you from where you are to where you want to be. It is not a cake walk I assure you. The results will be worth the effort and sacrifice.

So far, we have discussed the foundation of wealth accumulation, which starts with having a mini Rainy Day Fund of $500 - $1,500 saved for life's minor unexpected events; we also talked about preparing a Monthly Money Plan to control your money because if you do not control your money, it will leave you and have you wondering where it went. Third, we talked about getting rid of the dream killer (i.e., debt) to live a life free of all consumer debt by using the Debt Crusher Method. Then, we addressed increasing the Rainy Day Fund to three to nine months of living expenses. I want you to be ready for the storms of life! These elements are the foundation of wealth accumulation and must be established to move toward not being broke.

As we talk about accumulating wealth, I recommend doing the next action steps together: 1) Saving for retirement, 2) Saving for your children's college education, and 3) Crushing the home mortgage debt. That means, you will save for retirement, fund your kid's college education, and destroy the mortgage debt all at once.

This is the second stretch of the adventure. You have reached the halfway mark of the process, and I want to stop and congratulate you because you have made it this far! Congratulations! You can do this! Don't stop now, keep going! Are you ready for the second half of the journey to maximize your money to stop being broke? Let's go!

Dream Chasing: Retirement Planning

Many people may envision their retirement years being one of travel (domestic and abroad), spending time with family and friends, and having lots of money to spend. What is your vision of retirement? Do you have plans to travel to all fifty states in the United States of America? Or, do you desire to travel to Italy and visit Rome? Are you envisioning you and your spouse taking a cruise to St. Lucia or Montego Bay? Do you want to spend your years volunteering with a charitable organization of your choice? Or, do you see yourself visiting your children and grandchildren creating memorable moments that will last forever? I encourage you to visualize the life that you desire for retirement. Maybe you love your job or vocation so much that you want to continue to contribute to society by using your talents to enrich other people's lives. Let your imagination go wild! Put your dream in writing, share it, and take action to make it a reality.

Now that you have an idea of the dream that you want to live while in retirement, how much do you want to live on during retirement? Do you want to keep the same standard of living that you currently have, or do you want to increase or reduce it? How much will those trips to see your children and grandchildren cost you? How much will you need to meet your monthly expenses? There are so many questions to ask and variables to consider. Here is the ultimate question. Have you started planning for retirement?

Retirement is Coming Whether You Are Ready or Not

You have a dream of retiring comfortably, right? But how are you going to retire if you have not saved money? According to PwC, a quarter of US adults have no retirement savings.[1] If that is not a sobering statistic, I do not know what is. Sadly, many people have a false sense of their retirement. The reality is that those who have not prepared for retirement will be surprised when it arrives. Imagine, wanting to leave your day job after working thirty or forty years, but will have to continue to work because you did not properly plan for your golden years. Well, those golden years will not seem "golden" because you will still need to work to provide income to cover your basic needs. People may think that getting Social Security will be enough to supply sufficient income to maintain a certain standard of living. Social Security is not enough for someone to live a comfortable life.

Saving for retirement is very, very important. In fact, it must be a priority. Why? Because as mentioned before, depending on Social Security is not enough to afford you a comfortable living. You must take responsibility for your retirement. Your retirement is your responsibility, not the United States Federal government's responsibility. People may have delayed saving for retirement for various reasons such as putting other things above retirement, saving for their children's college tuition, or paying for their parent's medical expenses. Whatever the case may be, planning for retirement is urgent and important. It must be a priority because whether you like it or not, retirement is coming. It is your choice to plan (or not) for it. Be ready.

Retirement Planning 101: Investing for Your Future

Retirement savings starts with realizing the importance of saving money. Once you understand this concept, the next thing to do is understand what to invest in. Never buy something that you do not understand. I know this sounds like common sense, but trust me, I have made purchases without understanding what I was buying. Shameka and I needed to replace the bed in our apartment when we relocated to Tennessee. My wife found a furniture store in Nashville that had a great deal on a bed, or so we thought. I thought that the bed came with the box spring, mattress, and bed frame. Unfortunately, the salesperson did not disclose that the purchase only came with the mattress and box spring; the bed frame the box spring and mattress rest on was not part of the deal. I failed to ask the salesperson and did not completely review the invoice before making the purchase. So be informed about your purchases. Be informed about your investing decisions as well.

Mutual Funds: The Vehicle to Retirement

You may have heard of the term "stock market." I do not want you to be afraid of those two words. A stock market is just like a grocery store. You can buy a variety of items that may be on sale or that are high priced. When there is a food shortage, prices in the store generally increase, but when there is an overstock of items, they go on sale. A gallon of milk may be on sale during the summer months because not many people are drinking milk. However, during the winter months (or when there is a snow storm), people run to the grocery store in droves to get milk, eggs, and bread; in this situation, the price of milk will have increased due to the demand and the weather. By the way, I still do not understand the reason that people buy milk, eggs, and bread during snow storms. Well, the stock market is similar to a grocery store, or supermarket.

You can buy different investments in the stock market such as stocks, bonds, and other investments. An investor (you or me) can buy and sell investments that are on sale or may be high priced. The vehicle that is going to lead you to the destination of retirement is a mutual fund. A mutual fund is when a group of people pool their money together to invest in different securities, or investments. For example, if 100 people each put $1,000 in a fund of securities, that group would have "mutually" funded an investment; the fund's value would be $100,000. Hence, the investment would be a mutual fund because the 100 people mutually agreed to fund an investment. The fund's value increases as the overall price of stocks within the fund increases. If the value of the fund started at $100,000 and in five years the fund's value is $250,000, the fund value will have increased by $150,000.

The most common investment vehicles are stocks and bonds. Stocks represent ownership in a company. When an investor invests money in a company so that the company can raise capital to produce its goods and/or services, the investor becomes an "owner" in the business. For example, Sherry has purchased ownership in a packaging company and is now a "shareholder" because she owns shares, or pieces of ownership, in the company. If Sherry purchased 100 shares of stock for $100 and the price of the stock increases to $150, her investment would have increased by $50, or by 50%. The rate of return on the investment is 50%, which is a pretty good return on her original investment.

People also invest money in companies by loaning it in the form of bonds. A bond is a debt instrument used by companies to operate to provide its goods and services to customers. Companies issue bonds, or debt, to investors in exchange for money to run the daily operations and to meet other obligations. The investors receive interest payments for loaning the money for a certain period of time (e.g., five years) and will receive the original investment at the end of the lending period. For example, if you invested $2,000 in a company via a bond instrument for ten years at 5% interest, you would receive $8.33 in interest each month for ten years, or $1,000 in interest. When your bond matures, you would receive the $2,000 that you originally invested. Your investment would have earned you $1,000, or a 50% return on investment.

There are several guidelines that you should be aware of when investing. Here are the criteria for investing.
1) Never invest in anything you do not understand.
2) Gather as much information as possible.
3) Never invest in single stocks.
4) Only invest in stock mutual funds.
5) Work with an investment advisor that is professional, caring, and is willing to teach you about investing.

Never Invest In Anything You Do Not Understand

You want to make an informed decision when investing your money. Do not make a decision to buy a stock mutual fund if you are not sure what you are buying. If you cannot explain to someone else what the investment is, then I recommend not buying it.

Gather As Much Information As You Can

By gathering information about investing, you will be armed to make wise investment decisions. You will also be able to ask questions of your investment advisor to clarify any areas that are unclear to you.

Never Invest in Single Stocks

Investing in single stocks is risky. When you invest in single stocks, there is a possibility to lose your original investment because of the time commitment to researching the stocks. Unless you trade stocks on a daily basis, investing in single stocks requires lots of time researching various stocks and the stock market. Also, investing in single stocks is risky because it is similar to putting all of your eggs (i.e., money) in one basket. However, when you invest in stock mutual funds, your money will be spread among dozens or hundreds of stocks; thereby, lowering your risk of losing money.

Only Invest in Stock Mutual Funds

Again, when you invest in stock mutual funds, you reduce the risk of losing your investment. Your money is spread among many stocks, which is called diversification. Diversification is a fancy investment term that basically means to "spread around." In addition, when you invest in stock mutual funds you are able to purchase more investments when you pool your money with other investors than if you invested in single stocks.

Work with an Investment Advisor that Cares and Is Willing to Teach You

You should get information so that you are informed about investing. You should also find an investment professional that cares about your well-being, goals, family, and future and is willing to teach you about investing. Having an investment advisor that meets this description will benefit you in making wise financial decisions. An investment advisor can help you understand the investing process and guide you in making the best decisions to get you the results that you want for a comfortable retirement. The investment advisor will be a voice of reason when the media is declaring a financial meltdown in the stock market. That voice will give you the confidence to continue to invest in the stock market during down times. Remember, investing is for the long term (i.e., five years or longer). I suggest asking a trusted friend or someone you know to refer you to an investment advisor that she trusts. Interview at least three investment advisors to find one that you feel comfortable working with to build your financial future.

Now that you have the criteria for investing, you wonder what's next, right? Well, before making a purchase of a stock mutual fund, there are some other details that need to be addressed to help you make good investment decisions.

Objective: Direction for Your Investments

Every stock mutual fund has an objective or purpose. The purpose of the fund can be found in the fund's prospectus, which is a document that explains the information about the stock mutual fund; it is a great resource to help you in your investing journey. Some of the funds' objectives include growth, growth and income, and aggressive growth. For example, if a fund's objective is growth, the fund's primary purpose is to increase the fund's value. If you purchased a stock mutual fund that had a value of $10,000, and you invested for the long-term (i.e., five years of longer), the fund manager's job would be to increase the overall fund's value, which includes your $10,000 investment. Other funds may have an objective to provide growth and income. For this fund, the fund manager would seek to increase the fund's value and provide income through dividends. A dividend is the income produced by stock. If you invest in stock mutual funds, as an owner that has invested money into the fund, you receive dividends as a return on your investment, or ROI. If you invest in a bond mutual fund, you would receive income via interest payments. Remember, a bond is a debt instrument, so you would receive interest payments as ROI based on the interest rate specified on the bond.

Here is a list of the most common objectives for stock mutual funds and their descriptions.

Aggressive Growth: Invests primarily in stocks of companies whose values are expected to increase very fast; usually small companies.

Growth: Mutual funds with a growth objective invest in company stocks that have values that are expected to increase, but not as fast as aggressive growth mutual funds; growth mutual funds consist of middle-sized to large, established companies.

Growth and Income: This fund's objective seeks to increase the mutual fund's value and provide consistent income through dividends.

International /Foreign: Mutual funds with this objective invest in company stocks outside of the United States of America; the portfolio manager seeks to provide a return on the stockholders' money through the growth of the stocks' value.[2]

When investing, there is a level of risk that you are able to accept; the level of risk is called tolerance. There will be periods when the stock market will do really well, and there will be periods when it will perform very poorly. During those low times of performance, the value in your stock mutual fund may also decline. However, if your portfolio is well diversified, you will not have to worry about losing your entire investment because when the stock market is performing poorly, some of your investments will offset the funds that are not doing well. For example, if the international mutual fund's value plummets due to economic turmoil in China, then the growth stock mutual fund's value will offset the declining international mutual fund because its value will be increasing.

Can you accept the sharp declines in the stock market or are you uncomfortable with your portfolio losing value when the stock market takes a nose dive? Only you can answer those questions. When the stock market is down, it is prime time to invest more money. Why? Because you can buy more shares of stock at low prices in down times; think of it as a "sale." When things are on sale, you are able to buy at lower prices. It is the same concept with the stock market.

Do not exit the stock market by selling your investments when the market is declining. Fear can cause you to withdraw from the stock market. If you do, you will lose the ability to accumulate wealth because your money will no longer be "working for you." I encourage you to not do investing alone. As mentioned earlier, I suggest finding an investment advisor that will help guide you during this process. He will provide an objective perspective to help you clearly see that staying invested in the stock market is in your best interest.

We must know our risk tolerance, so that we will not let fear derail our investment plans. Investing is a long-term commitment.

Management: Stewards of Your Money

Portfolio managers are paid to manage, or oversee, the stock mutual funds. She usually has a team of managers that assist in selecting stocks for the mutual fund to meet the fund's objective. The portfolio manager and supporting team should have a good track record with the fund. On average, the portfolio managers and the team ideally should have about ten years of experience in the fund. Ten years of experience shows that the portfolio manager and the team have been through good and bad times in the stock market and have the knowledge, skills, and experience to overcome adversity.

Ensure that the stock mutual fund's portfolio manager and the fund's team have the prerequisite skills and knowledge to meet the fund's objective to help you retire comfortably.

Expenses

There are expenses associated with stock mutual funds. Expenses such as loads, or sales charges, are charged by the fund for buying and selling stocks within the fund. There are front loads and back loads, which are sales charges paid when buying and selling stocks. For one of my mutual funds, the front load is 5.75% when stocks are bought. Do not let the loads stop you from investing. If you are paying a 5% load for buying stocks in your stock mutual fund, compare the load amount to ROI; if you are earning 12% ROI for your stock return compared to the 5% load, you are earning 7% net of the load. There are stock mutual funds with no loads as well; however, the no load funds may have other fees that are more expensive than funds with loads.

In addition, there are annual operating fees charged for maintaining a stock mutual fund. These fees include management fees, distribution and service fees, and other fees. The portfolio managers are compensated for being stewards, or managers, of the stock mutual funds. They are paid via management fees, which are a percentage of the value of your investment. The management fee for one of my stock mutual funds is .38%.

The distribution and/or service fees, or 12b-1 fees, are marketing costs associated with the fund. The 12b-1 fee for one of my stock mutual funds is .24%. And, the other expenses make up the remaining costs charged by stock mutual funds. For my stock mutual fund, the other expense is .13%, which brings the total annual charges to .75%. The .75% is charged as a percentage of my investment (and would be for your stock mutual fund as well).

Volatility: How Much Are Your Investments Moving?

The stock market which is represented by the Standard and Poor's (S&P) 500 that consists of stocks of five hundred of the largest companies in the United States. The value of the stock market is massive! And, the S&P 500 reflects the performance of those stocks collectively. The value of those stocks is measured by what is called capitalization. Capitalization means dollar value. There are large capitalization, or cap, middle cap, and small cap stocks. The large cap stocks are stocks that have a market capitalization above $5 billion, mid-cap stocks have a market capitalization between $1 billion and $5 billion, and small cap stocks have a market capitalization below $1 billion.[3]

Large cap stocks are more stable than small and mid-cap stocks. The movement in stock market capitalization values refers to volatility, or price movement. The S&P 500 is known to increase and decrease daily, weekly, monthly, and annually. It can be similar to a roller coaster with its ups and downs. Stock prices are driven by various elements such as war, economic unrest, elections, weather, and other elements. Ultimately, the stock market is influenced by people's emotions. Think about this. If the stock market represents companies owned and operated by people (i.e., investors and stakeholders), those people's emotions (fears, doubts, worry, happiness, joy) affect the stock price of those companies. When people are afraid of the results of a presidential election, more than likely the stock market will decline because of the fear. Or, if there is a highly anticipated product that will be launched by a certain company, that company's stock price will likely increase because of the excitement about the new product.

Some other terms related to volatility are risk and return (or reward). When a stock is more volatile, it has a higher risk associated with the potential ROI. The reverse is true for stocks that are not very volatile; that means that the ROI is almost certain. However, the return will be low because the associated risk is low. Certificates of deposits (CDs) and checking accounts represent securities that have a low risk and low return.

A measure of a stock's volatility is called beta. Beta measures how much a stock's price increases or decreases in comparison to the S&P 500. A beta of 1 means that a stock's price moves with the stock market's value.[4] A beta of 1.5 indicates that a stock's price is 50% more volatile than the stock market. If a stock's beta is .75, it is 25% less volatile than the stock market. Make sure that you are able to handle the various price changes in your portfolio.

For long term investing, I recommend having a mixture of stock mutual funds in your portfolio.

Diversification
As mentioned earlier, when investing a good strategy to apply is diversification. Diversification means to spread around. You do not want to put all of your "eggs" in one basket. Diversification lowers the risk of you losing your investment. If you invest all of your money in one company, and the company files bankruptcy, you will have lost all of your money. However, if you invest your money in a stock mutual fund, that money will be invested in hundreds of companies reducing the risk of losing your money.

An example of not being diversified is the 2001 Enron scandal. As the Enron executives received millions of dollars in compensation, "lower-level employees were prevented from selling their stock [...] and many subsequently lost their life savings."[5] In addition, Enron filed bankruptcy and left "thousands of workers with worthless stock in their pensions."[6] The Enron scandal is a prime example for the need to diversify your investments. If the employees' pension offered various stock options within the plan, the employees would still have had their retirement savings. However, this was not the case. Lesson to be learned: Never put all of your investments in one stock; spread your money around to protect it from loss. Remember: Diversify, diversify, and diversify!

Stock Types

There are a variety of stock types for investing to further diversify your portfolio. Your investment advisor will have the option to invest in a money market account, stocks, bonds, or cash within your mutual fund. For long-term investing though, you want your money invested in stocks within the mutual fund. The fund manager will use the stocks within the mutual fund to create money for the investors.

Tax Favored Plans

In addition to putting your money into a stock mutual fund, there are other options available to you. The U.S. Federal government created several options through the Internal Revenue Code to allow taxpayers (you and me) to set money aside for retirement. What a treat! Congress created tax law in the Internal Revenue Code to give taxpayers an incentive to save for their retirement. Social Security alone is not enough for someone to live a dream retirement. It is YOUR responsibility to save for YOUR retirement! It's not your employer's responsibility or the government's responsibility to fund your retirement.

    The Internal Revenue Code specifies that certain investment plans get special treatment regarding taxes. Those investment plans with special tax treatment are called tax sheltered, or favored plans. The tax favored plans give taxpayers the ability to pay taxes later on certain investments or to pay taxes now and not pay taxes in the future. Let's look at some of the tax favored plans that can help you retire in style!

Individual Retirement Arrangement: An individual retirement arrangement (IRA), also known as a traditional IRA, is a savings plan for individuals. In the mainstream, the IRA is known as an individual retirement account, but it is really the individual retirement arrangement according to the Internal Revenue Code.[7] You and I can open a traditional IRA to invest money in for retirement. To qualify to open a traditional IRA, you must have taxable compensation (from working or self-employment) Prior to January 1, 2020, you were unable to contribute if you were age 70 ½ or older.[8]

    The advantages of a traditional IRA are that the contributions to the IRA are deductible on your tax return, so your contributions are not included in your annual income (i.e., it reduces the amount of tax you pay on your income), and the earnings and growth of your investment are not taxed until you withdraw the money. If you withdraw the money at age 65, you probably will pay less tax on the money because you may be in a lower tax bracket. Another advantage to the traditional IRA is that a non-working spouse can contribute to a his or her own IRA account. As long as the other spouse has earned income, the non-working spouse can invest in a traditional IRA; this feature is great for stay-at-home mothers and fathers. For 2021, you can invest $6,000 for the year and $7,000 if you are age 50 or older. Your spouse can also contribute to her own IRA ($6,000 or $7,000 if older than age 50).[9]

The traditional IRA also has some negative features. To prevent people from withdrawing their retirement funds early, there is a 10% penalty for withdrawing funds before age 59 ½. In addition to the early withdrawal penalty, you will have to pay taxes on the amount withdrawn at your regular tax rate. That means, if you are in a 15% tax bracket and $10,000 is taken out of your IRA before age 59 ½, you will pay 25% in taxes and penalties, or $2,500. Therefore, that $10,000 will soon be $7,500 ($10,000 minus $2,500). Lastly, your investment loses the ability to work for you to grow into a substantial amount when you make an early withdrawal from your traditional IRA.

Roth Individual Retirement Arrangement: A Roth IRA is similar to a traditional IRA. However, when you put money into a Roth IRA, you will be investing with after-tax dollars; that is, the money will already have income taxes taken out. The disadvantage to the Roth IRA is that contributions that you make to it will not reduce your current taxable income; but the major advantage to the Roth IRA is this same feature. When you withdraw the money in retirement, no taxes will be withheld because you will have already paid taxes in prior years. Your investment grows TAX FREE! That means that any increase in the value of your Roth IRA will not be taxed when you take the money out of the account. The Roth IRA is definitely a vehicle you want to use to lead you into the retirement of your dreams!

The contribution limit for the Roth IRA is the same as the traditional IRA.[10] There is no minimum distribution requirement (i.e.., withdrawals) like the traditional IRA.[11] In fact, the Roth IRA allows taxpayers to continue investing past age 70 ½. However, some people may not be able to contribute to a Roth IRA based on their income level. Consult a tax professional for more information about the income limitations.

In my opinion, the Roth IRA is superior to the traditional IRA because money invested in a Roth IRA grows TAX FREE. Therefore, I encourage you to make sure you include a Roth IRA in your retirement plan.

401(k) Plan: The 401(k) plan is probably one of the investing vehicles that most people know of. The Internal Revenue Service created the 401(k) plan, which is a plan that allows employers to set up an account for employees to voluntarily put money into the account for retirement.

401(k) gets its name from the Internal Revenue Code because it is section 401, subsection k of the Code.

Prior to the 401(k) plan, employers offered their employees a pension plan. Pensions are based on factors such as an employee's age, years of service, and other factors to determine the employee's retirement pension amount. The pension plans were more expensive for employers to maintain than a 401(k) plan as the employer was responsible for having enough money to cover the employees' pensions. Therefore, companies started offering their employees 401(k) plans and eliminating the pension plans. With pension plans, the employer took responsibility for the employees' retirement savings. The 401(k) plan relieved companies of this responsibility and gave employees the responsibility of saving for their own retirement.

The 401(k) allows employees to put before-tax dollars into an account for retirement. There is an $19,500 maximum contribution into the 401(k) for 2020.[12] You must be age 59 ½ to withdraw funds from the account.[13] If money is taken out of the 401(k) account before age 59 ½, a 10% penalty will be accessed, and you will pay taxes on the amount withdrawn at your regular tax rate as well.

Another advantage of the 401(k) plan is that some employers provide a matching incentive to encourage employees to save for retirement. Some employers may match, or contribute, a certain amount (e.g., dollar for dollar) to their employees' 401(k) plans. If you voluntarily have $100 withheld from your paycheck each pay period for retirement, your employer may contribute $100 into your 401(k) plan. Other companies may match their employees' contribution up to a certain percentage. For instance, when I worked for a debt buying company in South Carolina, the company matched a percentage of what I contributed to the 401(k) account. Shameka's current employer matches her 401(k) contributions up to 4%.

I want to offer two suggestions. The first suggestion is to never borrow money from your 401(k) plan. Let's say you borrow money from your 401(k) plan. Within that same month, you are terminated from your job (or you quit working). You will have to repay the amount borrowed within 30-60 days. The second suggestion is to put money into the 401(k) plan. If you do not put money into the account, then you will not have retirement savings. Again, saving for retirement is your responsibility, not your employer's or the government's.

Deferred Compensation Plan or 457 Plan: The deferred compensation plan, or 457 plan, is a retirement plan offered to state or local government entities.[14] Amounts can be contributed by the employee electing to defer compensation until a later date. Therefore, the employee is not currently taxed on amounts deferred; the employee will pay taxes on amounts deferred when money is withdrawn from the 457 plan. If you work for a state or local government agency, check to see if a 457 plan is available to you.

403(b) Plan*:* A 403(b) plan gets its name from the Internal Revenue Code section 403, subsection b. It is a qualified retirement plan for certain employees of public schools, employees of certain tax-exempt organizations, and certain ministers. If your employer offers a 403(b) plan, the most you can contribute to the account for 2020 and 2021 is $19,500.[15] There are penalties and additional taxes for early withdrawal of funds from a 403(b) plan, similar to a traditional IRA.

Simplified Employee Pension (SEP) Plan*:* A Simplified Employee Pension (SEP) plan is an arrangement that allows your employer to set up an account to make contributions for you for retirement. The contributions are deductible, which means they are not included in your current income; thus, reducing your current taxable income. However, you will pay taxes on the contributions when money is withdrawn from the SEP plan. The SEP has the same tax consequences and penalties as the other tax-favored plans, with the exception of being able to contribute to the SEP after age 70 ½.[16]

Which Vehicle Should You Drive for Your Retirement?
Now that we have discussed the ABCs of retirement savings, you may be asking, "Which plan or accounts do I choose for my retirement?" Great question! Here is what I suggest for investing.
1) Invest 10% to 15% of your income into tax-favored retirement plans and before and after-tax retirement plans.
Why is 10% to 15% suggested instead of a higher percentage? I recommend using that range of percentages for various reasons. First, other experts like Thomas Stanley, mention investing 15% of your income. Second, you will use your remaining income to continue moving toward other financial goals such as college funding and getting rid of your home mortgage.
2) Invest in four types of stock mutual funds:
- 1/4 of your income in Growth Stock Mutual Fund
- 1/4 of your income in Growth and Income Stock Mutual Fund
- 1/4 of your income in Aggressive Growth Stock Mutual Fund
- 1/4 of your income in International/Foreign Stock Mutual Fund
3) Investing Strategy

- *First*, invest in your employer's tax favored plan (i.e., 401(k), 403(b), 457, or SEP) up to the employer's matching contribution (invest even if your employer does not offer a matching contribution).
- *Second*, invest the maximum amount into a Roth IRA (if your employer does not offer a retirement plan, start your investing with a Roth IRA).
- *Lastly*, invest the remaining amount into your employer's tax favored plan to achieve the suggested 10% - 15% figure.

The Power of Compound Interest

We have discussed the different types of investments and what to invest in, let's talk about how investing will allow you to make your money work for you. Earlier we discussed that you are the boss of your money via budgeting. With investing, compound interest makes your hard-earned money work for you to make your retirement dream come true. Compound interest is a mathematical equation that causes a financial explosion that gives your money the fuel it needs to grow exponentially! With compound interest, your original investment earns interest, then the original investment and interest combined earns interest, and the process continues causing your money to grow! The result of compound interest is not 1+1=2; it's 1+1=3. Here is a story to illustrate the power of compound interest.

Two sisters, Roxanne and Desiree, both graduated from high school and began working. Roxanne started a job after high school and began to invest in a stock mutual fund at age 20. She invested $1,000 a year in a stock mutual fund at age 20 until age 27, and then she stopped investing at age 27. She had invested $8,000 and did not add to her account. At age 65, Roxanne's stock mutual fund balance was $1,021,874! Wow! On the other hand, Desiree started investing $1,000 a year from age 27 to age 65 giving her a total investment of $38,000. At age 65, Desiree's stock mutual fund balance was $683,010. That's a $338,863 difference compared to Roxanne's balance! If Desiree put more money in her account than Roxanne (i.e., $38,000 versus $8,000), why does Roxanne have more money than Desiree? Because Roxanne started investing before Desiree, Roxanne's money had more time to grow than her sister's. Compound interest works best when you start investing early. The moral of the story: Start investing early so that compound interest can make your money work harder and grow faster.

If you have not started investing for retirement and are in your 30s, 40s, or 50s, do not panic or despair. There is hope for you! It is never too late to start saving for retirement. You may be starting late in the game, but better late than never, my friend. You may have to reduce your current lifestyle to make the necessary sacrifices to save for retirement.

Or, you may have to increase your income to accelerate the process, but you can make the necessary changes to retire comfortably.

Follow these steps outlined before investing: 1) Save a $500 - $1,500 for your mini Rainy Day Fund; 2) Create your Monthly Money Plan; 3) Destroy your consumer debt using the Debt Crusher Method; and 4) Increase your Rainy Day Fund to three to nine months of living expenses. Once you have followed those steps, then you are ready to start funding your retirement dream and move toward accumulating wealth.

Retirement Savings for Military Members

Before I start this section, I want to show my gratitude for the military members in the United States Armed Forces. If you currently serve or have served in the military, I want to thank you for serving this great nation. Freedom comes with sacrifice; thank you for sacrificing your life for millions of Americans.

I have family members that serve or have served in the military. One of my great uncles served in one of the World Wars. While in the military, he got frost bite and eventually had to have one of his legs amputated. He lived with my grandmother, his sister, when I was in high school. My uncle was a disabled veteran. I do not know if he had a retirement plan established while in the military. I doubt that he did because he came to live with my grandmother. Did my uncle fail to plan for retirement, or did he plan to fail by not preparing for it? I want you to know that I care about your retirement dream! I do not want you to depend on your Social Security check. That's not enough money for you to live your dream retirement. As a member of the military, here is what you can do to reach your retirement goals.

Thrift Savings Plan*:* The Thrift Savings Plan (TSP) is a government sponsored retirement plan for military members. Congress created the TSP through the Federal Employees' Retirement Act of 1986. The TSP is similar to a 401(k) plan with its tax advantages such as members' ability to deduct contributions from current income. Another perk of the TSP is that members can contribute to a Roth TSP, which means that military members can contribute after-tax dollars to the account just like a Roth IRA.[17] Therefore, when you take the money out in retirement, you will not pay taxes because taxes will already have been withheld. Your investment grows TAX-FREE with the Roth TSP! For 2021, the maximum amount that can be contributed to a TSP account is $19,500. The TSP account gives military members the ability to diversify their investment. There are six investment options available to invest in a TSP.

- Government Securities Investment Fund (G Fund): Invests in low-risk investments like U.S. Treasury bonds.

- Fixed Income Investment Fund (F Fund): Invests in the bond market, which provide investment returns in the form of interest payments.
- Common Stock Investment Fund (C Fund): This fund invests in common stocks in the S&P 500; there is more risk associated with this fund, but there is more reward, or ROI.
- Small Cap Investment Fund (S Fund): The "S Fund" invests in small cap stocks that are not part of the S&P 500; this fund is riskier than the "C Fund" because the companies do not have an established track record of performance, but they have great growth potential.
- International Investment Fund (I Fund): You guessed it! This fund buys stock of international companies in Europe, Africa, and the Far East; this fund by far has the most risk because it is investing in companies outside of the United States where there may be uncertain economic conditions within the countries that stocks are held.
- Life Cycle Investment Fund (L Fund): The "L Fund" is a mixture of all the other funds (i.e., G, F, C, S, and I); its investment strategy focuses on the time horizon (i.e., the retirement age or investment withdrawal date) of military members; as members approach their time horizon, the money is put in the more conservative funds (i.e., the G and F Funds).[17]

The six funds are not actively managed, which means they are not managed by a portfolio manager. Money is invested into the funds, and the funds' performance replicates benchmark indexes. Therefore, these funds' performance mirrors their respective indexes such as the S&P 500 or the Dow Jones Industrial Average (DJIA). The S&P 500 and DJIA are not managed by a portfolio manager, so they are passively managed.

Those are the investment options available to military members; here is the recommended investing strategy.
- Invest 50% in the "C Fund"
- Invest 25% in the "S Fund"
- Invest 25% in the "I Fund"

The TSP is just like the other investment options that we have discussed so far. If you do not put money into it, you will not get much out of it. I want you to have the best retirement possible. However, it is your responsibility to save for your retirement. Just like you sacrifice yourself in the military defending the lives of millions of people in America, I want you to sacrifice for your retirement. You can do it!

Action Steps to Maximize Your Money to Stop Being Broke
1. Find an investment professional that cares for you, your family, and goals and is willing to teach you about the investing process.
2. Invest 10% to 15% of your take home income in pre-tax and after-tax retirement plans and tax-favored retirement plans.

Multi-Tasking for a Prosperous Future
Retirement, College Savings, and Mortgage Crushing
Task 2: College Savings

In 1999, I became the first high school graduate in my immediate family. My family was proud of my accomplishment. I was stoked as well! Neither of my parents finished high school, so they were happy that I decided to earn my diploma. I grew up in a low-income family, and my parents did not have the money to send me to college. After graduation I enrolled in a local community college in my hometown. I did not have a career path selected, but I knew that I did not want to be low income for the rest of my life. I enrolled in the college's welding program. Since I did not know what I wanted to do for a career, my goal was to study something that would take a short amount of time to complete so that I could get a job making money. The college awarded me grants to attend school. Therefore, I did not get student loans to pay for my tuition; I lived at home with my parents, so I did not have to pay for room and board.

I took classes full time and worked full time at a pharmaceutical company that manufactured vitamins and supplements. As a natural "Saver," I saved money while in school. While attending a psychology in the workplace course, the psychology professor, Montina Wesley, saw potential in me as I was one of her high performing students. One day she asked me, "What are you doing studying welding? You should be majoring in business, not welding." The discussion led her to contact someone in the college's TRIO program, which is a program that helps people from disadvantaged backgrounds. The TRIO program contact connected me with a college in Kentucky. The college in Kentucky is unique because its students are mainly from low-income families and disadvantaged backgrounds.

In addition, the college gives students the opportunity to go to college tuition-free! The college's endowment, funds provided to the college by donors and investments, provides the resources to pay for the students' tuition; although students are responsible for paying their room and board. I applied to the college and got accepted to attend.

In the summer of 2001, I became the first person in my immediate family to earn an associate's degree. And, in August 2001 I embarked on a journey for a bachelor's degree at the college in Kentucky. Again, I received grants to pay for most of my room and board. The college had a mandatory labor program that required students to work on campus while going to school. I worked ten hours each week in addition to completing my studies. I enjoyed attending college. It's where my wife, Shameka, and I met.

Because of the college's tuition-free policy, my strong work ethic, and gifts from generous people, in May 2005 I graduated with a bachelor's degree in business administration almost debt free! I owed the school about $1,000; the debt was not for student loans, but for a medical procedure performed on me for braces on my teeth. Once I got a "real" job after college I repaid the debt.

I was blessed to attend two colleges without incurring thousands of dollars of student loan debt. I received grants to pay for college, AND I worked while in school. It is possible to go to college and graduate debt free.

The second phase of wealth accumulation is funding your children's college. My parents did not save for my college education. It was my responsibility to pay for college. Shameka and I recently had our first child, Naomi Desiree, and we plan to prepare for her college education. Saving for your child's education is an investment in them. In order for us to prepare for our children's education, we need to know what options are available.

Education Savings Account: The Coverdell Education Saving Account, or ESA, is an investment account used for saving for education expenses. The contributions for the ESA are not tax deductible; however, the contributions grow TAX FREE (we like free!) until funds are withdrawn. The maximum contribution into an ESA is $2,000 per year. So if you invest $2,000 for eighteen years, then your total investment will be $36,000. That ESA will have grown to $99,328![1] $63,328 is growth. It pays to invest in an ESA for your kids' college education because of the growth potential that could help them graduate debt free!

In addition, the money must be spent on qualified expenses for higher education, secondary, or elementary education. Your child must be younger than age 18 to establish an ESA for him. Funds can be used for the child's tuition, books, room and board, and other qualifying expenses. For higher education and post-secondary education (i.e., vocational school), students must be enrolled at least half-time to use the ESA for education expenses.[2] There are income limitations for contributing to an ESA, so consult with a tax professional for more information.

Imagine your child earning a bachelor's degree and leaving college with no "ball and chain" attached to her leg. As of June 2021, student loan debt was $1.57 TRILLION![3] (That is a lot of debt!). In other words, students are graduating college with a tremendous amount of student loan debt. We must be proactive in preparing for our children's education. Investing in the ESA will assist in the preparation.

529 Plan: A 529 plan, or Qualified Tuition Plan, is another option available for saving for college education. With the 529 plan, you can either prepay or contribute to an account for your child's qualified education expenses. Contributions or prepayments are not deductible, but distributions from the 529 plan are tax free if the distribution does not exceed the qualified education expense. The 529 plan pays for either qualified higher education expenses or qualified elementary and secondary education expenses.[4] In addition, you can contribute up to the amount of the student's qualified education expenses, but not more than that amount. There is no income restriction on a 529 plan, so anyone can contribute to the plan. A 10% penalty is assessed on non-education distributions.[5] You and I can save money in both an ESA and a 529 plan at the same time for the same child. Pretty cool!

When you invest in a 529 plan, your money will be invested in mutual funds and managed by a fund manager. There are a couple of options available via a 529 plan. The first option will invest your money based on the child's time horizon (i.e., time he plans to attend college). As the time horizon approaches, the money will be invested in less risky investments (beginning with stocks and then invests in bonds and cash). The second investment option will invest your money in cash-like investments such as money market funds and insurance backed guaranteed funds. These investments do not keep pace with inflation, so I do not recommend investing money in these investments for your 529 plan.[6] I do not recommend selecting the time horizon option either because you want to be in control of the investments, not let a computer automatically modify your investments. You and I want to maximize the investment's potential to grow as much as possible.

Lastly, I do not recommend prepaying for your child's education. Why? Because the prepayment only covers the amount of tuition, not room, board and other costs.[7] And, if the price of education increases, which it will, you will have to pay more to cover the additional expenses.

College Rules: Ways to Go to College Debt Free

Are you convinced yet that going to college without going into debt is possible? If not, let's continue our discussion. As we have seen, there are ways to eliminate the need to borrow money for college education using the ESA and 529 plan. I have more ways to show you how you and your child can plan for a debt free college experience. Here's how.

1) *College choice: In-state versus out of state; community college before four-year college*

When I went back to college in 2009 to earn a second bachelor's degree with an accounting emphasis, I took the prerequisite classes at a community college. At that time, I received state funding to pay for most of my tuition and books. I took classes for about a year before transferring to a four-year university to finish my degree. Both institutions were in-state, so I did not have to pay out-of-state tuition.

College choice is a major factor in the cost of your child's college education. In 2019, the average in-state tuition and other costs (room and board) to attend a public, four-year institution in the United States was $20,598. The out-of-state tuition, room, and board for that same year, was $26,382.[8] So your child would pay an additional $5,784 to attend an out-of-state college or university. That's just for one year. Multiply the $20,598 for in-state costs by four, and your child's education would cost $82,392; the out-of-state cost would be $105,528! That's over $100,000 for a college education! We do not want our children to graduate with this much student loan debt. That is the reason for you and me to plan for our kids' college.

I recommend guiding your child to make the right choice for attending college. As parents, it is our responsibility to help our children make good decisions. I suggest helping your child identify an area of study that interests her and that has economic value (i.e., a career or vocation that will provide a sustainable income). Your child may or may not know an area to study; by asking, "What do you enjoy doing? If money were not an issue, what would you do for a living," your child will begin to think about different career or vocation options. Once your child has identified an area of study, I recommend her attending a local community college to take the prerequisite courses necessary to pursue a bachelor's degree (if your child decides to take this path). By attending a community college, your child will be able to take the prerequisite courses at a lower price. She will pay more per credit hour for those same courses at a four-year institution.

In addition, the community college may have a program that allows students to transfer the credits to a four-year institution. When I pursued my second bachelor's degree, I took classes at a local community college and transferred those credit hours to a four-year university. I did it, so can your child!

2) *Work: It won't kill your child!*

I worked part-time at a car wash for about two and a half years while in high school. I did not get to go to many high school football and basketball games because I worked. However, I had money. I bought my first car while in high school. My grades were not that good the first couple of years of high school, but I improved them my junior and senior years. Although I worked, I still completed my school assignments.

When I pursued my associate's degree in welding, I worked full-time at a pharmaceutical company as a material handler and worked on an assembly line AND went to school full-time. I took classes in the morning and worked second shift from about 2:30 p.m. until 10:30 p.m. Then after graduating with my associate's degree, I pursued my bachelor's degree in Kentucky. While in college in Kentucky, I worked in the shipping and receiving department and later worked at the college's library. Then, when I pursued my second bachelor's degree, I worked part-time at a pizza restaurant delivering pizzas and beverages to customers, and then later worked at a public library in my hometown.

There is a common theme in this section: WORK! Each time I pursued a college education, I worked. Working did not cause my grades to suffer. I may have sacrificed participating in extracurricular activities, but my grades were fine, and I helped pay for my education.

Lastly, according to Shannon Vasconcelos, director of college finance at Bright Horizons College Coach, "Students who work a moderate amount of hours— up to fifteen, maybe twenty hours a week) — those students actually on average do better in school than students who don't work at all."[9]

3) *Scholarships (SAT and ACT scores)*

One thing that I hated in school was taking timed tests! I really disliked timed tests because I took too much time completing them. I am a perfectionist; I overanalyzed (and still overanalyze) questions on tests because I wanted to get the right answer. I am very driven, and when I was in school, I strived to get an "A" on my assignments, which led me to overanalyze when test taking.

I took both the SAT (Scholastic Assessment Test) and the ACT (American College Test) in high school. Both tests are standardized tests that assess your knowledge of reading, writing, English, and math. Students take the tests for entrance into college. I did not score well on the SAT; I think I had better scores on the ACT, which allowed me to get accepted into the local community college in my hometown. I received grants, or money provided by the government, to pay for my college education when I pursued my associate's degree and first bachelor's degree. Grants do not have to be repaid, unlike student loans. I recommend that you encourage your child to prepare for and take both the SAT and ACT tests. He can get free material to take a practice exam for the ACT. The higher the test scores, the more money is awarded in scholarships. What is a scholarship? A scholarship is money that is awarded by the U.S. Federal government, state, or institution to pay for college education. Students that receive scholarships do not have to repay the money awarded (similar to a grant). Student loans are different than scholarships. Student loans must be repaid. If student loans are not repaid, your child (or you if you co-sign for the loan) could be sued and have your wages garnished for not paying. I advise not getting student loans to pay for your child's college education.

In addition, your child can do online research to find scholarships to pay for college. He could also get a book of scholarships from your local public library. Your child may have to prepare essays to compete for the scholarships. He may be able to get a scholarship for various reasons such as being economically disadvantaged or for declaring a specific area of study. I recommend your child spending spring and summer breaks from school searching for and applying for scholarships to help fund his college education. It's essentially free money (with the exception of some sweat equity!) for school.

4) *Internships while in college (help pay for college and get experience)*
When I attended college in Kentucky, I applied for an internship. Some internships may not offer pay (monetarily), but provide valuable work experience. I did an internship with a non-profit organization in Washington, D.C. to help small businesses gain access to funding and other resources. I had a chance to work alongside two international students going to various businesses to inform them of our services. Specifically, I assisted a client that owned a restaurant with getting the necessary items (i.e., utensils, cutlery, and burners) for an annual festival held at the National Mall. The experience enriched my life! I improved my work ethic, visited Washington, D.C., helped people, AND received payment while doing so!

An internship is another avenue for your child to pay for his college education. Getting an internship is just as competitive as getting a scholarship, so encourage him to seek internships before and during college. An internship will expose your child to a field and allow him to find out whether or not the profession is suitable for him.

5) *Compare on-campus vs off-campus expenses*
I lived on campus all four years while pursuing my first bachelor's degree. Living in a dormitory, or dorm, gave me exposure to a community that I would not have had otherwise. Shameka and I both lived in dorms. We ate at the college's food service. We did not really need to cook a meal unless we wanted to cook. I did not have a car on campus, so I rode the shuttle van, rented a car from the college, and rode with other students to go places. I paid my on-campus expenses, or room and board (dorm and meals), each semester via my term bill.

If I had lived off-campus, I would have had to pay rent for housing, food, utilities, car insurance, maintenance, gas for my car, and laundry. Although I worked on campus ten hours each week, my monthly living expenses would probably have exceeded my monthly income. Therefore, if I would have compared living on-campus versus off-campus, living on-campus would have been more beneficial and economical for a broke college student like me.

We need to help our children compare the costs of living on-campus versus off-campus. If your child is going to pay for some of the expenses, it is important to evaluate the costs and create a Monthly Money Plan for him. This process will help your child live within his means, which will establish a habit of budgeting that will be used after he graduates college. Here are a few questions to ask when comparing costs.

- How much is room and board each semester compared to off-campus monthly expenses?
- How much money will your child earn each month?
- Can your child get another job to cover off-campus expenses?
- What expenses will your child be responsible for paying?
- Will your child develop better relationships with other students living on-campus versus being isolated from community while living off-campus?
- Will your child have healthier food choices living on-campus than off-campus?
- Will your child be distracted living off-campus rather than on-campus?

Sending your child to college without getting student loans is possible. I believe that if you and your child follow the steps outlined above, you will be able to leave your child a legacy that has the potential to change your family for generations. I do not want your child to drop out of college for lack of money for college. In fact, according to the New York Times, "Money is the number one reason students give when they drop out [of college]."[10] Let's work hard to not let our children be victims to this statistic.

Action Steps to Maximize Your Money to Stop Being Broke
1. Talk to a professional investment advisor about setting up an ESA and 529 plan for your children's college education. Make sure you 1) understand, and then 2) fund the account.
2. Encourage your child to prepare for the SAT and ACT tests. Help her understand the importance of earning good grades to get accepted into college.
3. Talk to your child about work, searching for internships, scholarships, and grants to pay for college. Encourage her to apply for internships, scholarships, and grants early.

Multi-Tasking for a Prosperous Future
Retirement, College Savings, and Mortgage Crushing
Task 3: Mortgage Crushing

Home Ownership

Home ownership is part of the American Dream. Owning a home represents stability, safety, and security. Home provides shelter from the storms of life. Home ownership gives us the freedom to establish roots in a community that we can build relationships with other people. Community enriches our lives. Home allows us to open up to other people by inviting them for dinner, meet to connect with other fellow followers of Christ, and to create memorable moments at holidays, birthdays, and wedding anniversaries. Having a home is more than about providing shelter for your family; it's about developing relationships that start within the four walls of your home and extend out into the larger community. Home is about creating traditions that will last for generations to come.

Buying a home is a big responsibility. Owning a home is not like renting a house, condominium, or apartment. When you rent, you are not responsible for a lot of the repairs for the facility or property taxes. For example, if you rent an apartment and the dishwasher stops working, you can call the landlord to have it repaired. Or, if the seal on the balcony door needs replacing, the maintenance technician will come and replace the seal. On the other hand, when you own a home, you are responsible for the repairs. When you own a home and the heating and air conditioning unit malfunctions, you will have to replace it or pay someone else to fix the problem for you. If you are a "do-it-yourself" kind of person you may reduce the cost of paying someone to make repairs to your home by doing the repair yourself. However, the time involved to fix the problem may outweigh the alternative of calling a repair person.

The primary reason I discussed having a mega Rainy Day Fund is to protect you from life's hiccups when you buy a house. What if you and your spouse just closed on a house, and three months later the washer and dryer stop working? Well, if you have a mega Rainy Day Fund of three to nine months of living expenses, you will be able to replace those appliances with no sweat to your financial life. Having $10,000 to $30,000 set aside for unexpected events brings you and your family peace of mind when you purchase a home. However, if you buy a house with no savings and an appliance stops working, you won't be prepared for the event and more than likely revert back to your old habit of depending on debt to save you from your financial woes. That is why it is very important to have your mega Rainy Day Fund in place when you decide to buy a home.

Basics for Home Buying

Before we discuss the home buying process, let's set some ground rules to help us make wise purchasing decisions. First, we need to have our mini Rainy Day Fund of $500 - $1,500. Second, we need to do a Monthly Money Plan. Third, we should be completely debt free from consumer debt (i.e., no credit cards, car loans, student loans, or other debts). Fourth, we should have our mega Rainy Day Fund of three to nine months of living expenses. Then, we are investing 10% to 15% of our take home earnings in 401(k), traditional and Roth IRAs, and other tax favored retirement plans and saving for our children's college education. After all of those action steps have been taken, we will begin crushing the mortgage debt. (We will multi-task by saving for retirement, saving for children's college education, and destroying the mortgage debt at the same time). If you have not followed the process outlined above, I recommend re-reading the previous chapters, plan, and execute the plan to get to this part of the process. I want you to buy a home; I am on your side. I just want you to maximize your money to get the house, keep it, and not have financial despair. Here are the foundation steps to take to purchase your dream home.

Foundation Step #1: Pay Cash

I will be honest with you; I hate debt! I hate it with a vengeance! Why? As I mentioned before, debt is a thief. It can steal, kill, and destroy your hopes and dreams. Getting a loan to purchase a house means that you are borrowing money over a long period of time and are committing to repaying that money (with interest) to a lender. During that time, you could be using that money to build your dream retirement or accumulating massive amounts of wealth. Consider saving cash to purchase a home. Wow! What a thought. What if you could save $30,000 a year, or $2,500 a month, for five years? You would have saved $150,000! Imagine going to a custom home builder with a briefcase filled with $100 dollar bills. The builder tells you that the cost of the house would be $215,000. As the builder ends his statement, you tell him that you want to have a home built and that you are paying cash; then, you open the briefcase to show him the crisp stacks of $100 dollar bills. His mouth drops to the floor as his eyes glaze over. More than likely, the builder would build the house for a lower price because money "talks" especially $150,000 of "Benjamin Franklins."

Foundation Step #2: 15 Year Mortgage

Alright, so you have not been convinced to pay cash for a house. For those of you that are convinced....go for it! For the unconvinced group, the other option for home buying is to purchase a home with a fifteen year, fixed-rate mortgage that is no larger than 25% of your take-home earnings. That payment includes principal, interest, homeowner's insurance, and property taxes. Some people that I know have a home mortgage, but not a fifteen-year mortgage; they have a thirty-year mortgage. Who wants to be in debt for 30 YEARS? I don't! And, I don't want you to be either. Here's why. When you get a thirty-year mortgage, you will pay more interest over time than you would with a fifteen-year mortgage. Let me illustrate an example.

Shawn and Marcia buy their first home by getting a thirty-year mortgage for $200,000 at a fixed interest rate of 5.5%. Their monthly mortgage payment (principal and interest) would be $1,135. After thirty years, Shawn and Marcia would have a paid for home and would have paid $208,808 in interest. On the contrary, Langston and Jean decide to apply for a fifteen year, fixed-rate mortgage (with a 5.5% interest rate) with a monthly payment of $1,634. Langston and Jean's monthly payment is about $500 more than Shawn and Marcia's. However, after fifteen years, Langston and Jean would have a paid for house and will have only paid $94,150 in interest. Although Shawn and Marcia's monthly payment is lower, the couple paid $114,658 more in interest. That's the cost of getting a thirty-year mortgage! Langston and Jean will be able to save more money because they got a fifteen-year mortgage.

Foundation Step #3: 10% or 20% Down Payment

If you are not paying 100% cash for your home and are getting a fifteen year, fixed-rate mortgage, I recommend saving a 10% or 20% down payment for your home. When you have a down payment on the mortgage, it does three things for you: 1) Lets the lender know that you are serious about owning a home and want to reduce the risk of default, or not paying the mortgage, 2) reduces the length of time you have a mortgage on your home, and 3) alleviates the private mortgage insurance (PMI) requirement. PMI is insurance that protects the lender from a borrower that does not pay the mortgage. By having a 20% down payment, PMI is not required because it lowers your loan balance. For example, if the value of your home is $100,000 and you put a $20,000 down payment, the loan balance would be $80,000. Therefore, you would have a loan-to-value (LTV) of 80% ($80,000/$100,000=80%). So that means that 80% of the home's value is financed with debt.

The more money you put down when buying a home, the better. Some programs for first time home buyers may offer people the opportunity to purchase a home with no money down. I do not recommend purchasing a home with no money down because that would put your and your family's livelihood at stake having your home 100% leveraged with debt, which increases your risk 100% as well! I recommend at least a 10% or 20% down payment with a mega Rainy Day Fund to make your home a "dream" experience instead of a "nightmare" experience.

Mortgage Options: The Good, Bad, and Ugly

Buying a home is one of the biggest financial decisions that you will probably ever make. Homeownership should be an exciting process. In my family, there are several people that have bought homes or attempted to buy a house (I will discuss this later in more detail). There will be some stress in the home buying process, but I want to help alleviate some of the frustration associated with the process and make it a memorable and pleasant experience.

Before we move forward with the mortgage options, I want to pause for a moment to give some words of caution. Thus far, we have talked about some very important steps to take before buying a home. I highly suggest following the steps outlined in this and previous chapters. Why? Because I want you to own a home without the strain that occurs when you are not properly prepared. Let me illustrate my point.

I coached a single mother that had a son in college. My client owned a home and wanted to keep it for the security of her and her son. She attended one of my seminars and was interested in financial coaching. We met and discussed her situation. One of the glaring issues that she faced was losing her home in foreclosure. My wife and I coached our client and gave her the tools to create a budget and a debt elimination plan so that she would be armed to fight to keep her home. However, my client decided to file bankruptcy (which is an option, but not one that I recommend doing) to protect her from losing her home. If my client would have followed the steps I have outlined in this book before buying her home, she probably would not have filed bankruptcy.

Now that we have laid the foundation for purchasing a home, I want to discuss the mortgage options available to you. There are good and bad mortgage options. I want to arm you with the knowledge to make the best decision possible when buying the largest asset that you will ever purchase: a house.

Federal Housing Administration

The Federal Housing Administration, or FHA, is a private corporation that insures loans financed by homeowners. FHA loans give borrowers the opportunity to own a home with a down payment of 3.5%.[1] That means that the borrower's LTV is 96.5%, which means that the home is financed mostly with debt. Thus, FHA loans are risky because it allows borrowers to own a home with little money down. Also, FHA loans require borrowers to purchase PMI if a 20% down payment is not presented when buying the home, thereby, increasing the monthly mortgage payment. FHA loan guidelines are not as stringent as conventional loan guidelines, which allow more people to qualify for home loans.

Veterans Affairs

A VA loan is backed by the U.S. Department of Veterans Affairs, or VA; the loan itself, which can be used to purchase or refinance a home, isn't made by the government. Banks, mortgage companies, credit unions, and other kinds of mortgage lenders offer them. VA loans are only available to veterans, active-duty military and their surviving spouses. The VA insures borrowers' loans with no money down. Although the borrower is not required to have a down payment for the loan, the VA charges a funding fee, which could range between 1.4% to 3.6%.[2]

Conventional Mortgage

A conventional mortgage is a loan that conforms to guidelines set by the Federal Home Loan Mortgage Corporation (Freddie Mac) and the Federal National Mortgage Association (Fannie Mae). Conventional loans are not insured by the government, so borrowers are required to get PMI if they have a down payment of less than 20%.[3] Again, PMI protects the lender from the risk of the borrower not repaying the loan.

Also, conventional mortgages generally have lower costs than FHA, VA, and USDA loans.[4] Of the three types of home mortgages, a conventional mortgage is better because:
1) Lower interest rate compared to other loan options.
2) Required down payment of 20%, which lowers your chance of default and reduces the time you have a loan.

We just discussed the "good" options available to you for buying a home. I hope this information will serve you well. I also encourage you to use this information and get more knowledge so that you are informed about the home buying process. In life there is always a bad side or dark side. Mortgages are no exception. Let's talk about the "bad and ugly" mortgage options that I want you to stay away from and be aware of.

Adjustable Rate Mortgage

The cousin of the fixed-rate mortgage is the adjustable-rate mortgage, or ARM. A "fixed" rate mortgage does not change during the life of the loan. The ARM does change; hence, the name "adjustable" rate mortgage, which means that the interest rate will adjust or change during the term of the loan. When someone gets an ARM, the introductory interest rate is usually low. However, lenders will offer borrowers a low interest rate up front in exchange for a rate that will adjust up, or increase, over time. That means your mortgage payment will increase over time causing you to have a higher payment, which may cause you to lose your home. An ARM is a very, very bad (and ugly I might add) mortgage option for borrowers. I personally know a couple that had an ARM. Here's their story.

Alex and Kendra (their real names have been changed to protect their privacy) purchased a home in a suburb of my hometown. The couple became the first people in their immediate family to move toward homeownership. I spent time with this couple in their home making memorable moments. We would stay up late laughing, joking, playing games, and talking in their home. One memorable moment is a birthday party for two of my twin brothers. My parents, other siblings, cousins, aunt, uncle, and my in-laws attended the party. It was a fabulous party!

As we were creating lasting moments with this couple, their "dream" home was really a "nightmare." Why was it a nightmare? Because they had an ARM. The ARM increased so much that they could not afford to pay the mortgage payment. Eventually, they lost their home in foreclosure. The moral to this story: Do not get an adjustable rate mortgage.

Balloon Mortgage

Balloons are used in celebrating birthday parties, festivals, and other uplifting and encouraging events. Well, a balloon mortgage is far from bringing joy to a borrower. A balloon mortgage is a short-term loan (usually five-to-seven-year terms) that has a payment schedule similar to a thirty year, fixed-rate mortgage. Therefore, the monthly payments are the same for the duration of the loan period. After seven years of making monthly payments, the balance of the loan, or the "balloon" payment, is due.[5] Let's look at an example of a balloon payment.

Jerry and Annette get a $220,000 seven-year balloon mortgage based on a thirty year, fixed-rate mortgage with a 4% interest rate. The monthly payment is $1,050. At the end of the seven years, Jerry and Annette would have paid $57,557 in interest, and the remaining balance (i.e., balloon payment) of $189,330 would be due in full. If Jerry and Annette do not have the money to pay the balance, they would either have to sell their home or refinance the mortgage into a traditional mortgage.

More than likely, the couple would not have the money to pay the balance and would probably lose their home. The "balloon" would explode and cause havoc and chaos in their lives!

Reverse Mortgage

When something goes in reverse, it moves backward, right? A car can go in reverse; people may want to have a do-over and go in reverse to change their past. One thing that should not go in reverse is a mortgage. A reverse mortgage is a mortgage that allows borrowers, usually people age 60 and older, to borrow money against the value of their home. The borrower does not make payments, but receives money either in installments or a lump sum. When the borrower moves out of the house or dies, the balance owed (principal and accrued interest) is due.[6] Wow!

Imagine Leroy and Cheyenne are 65 years of age, retired, and have a paid for house worth $240,000. It took them thirty years to repay the original loan. Leroy and Cheyenne no longer work and receive Social Security benefits. A friend tells them about a reverse mortgage, and they decide to apply for a mortgage. They want to increase their monthly income by receiving payments from the reverse mortgage. Leroy and Cheyenne get approved for the reverse mortgage and are well on their way to a better quality of life. Then, five years later Leroy passes away, and Cheyenne goes into an assisted living facility. And, the remaining balance owed on the reverse mortgage is due. How will Cheyenne be able to pay the money owed? She will have to repay the loan through her estate (i.e., any assets owned by the couple) after she passes. I do not want you to become a victim of a reverse mortgage. I recommend running away from a reverse mortgage!

More Mortgage Mania: Title Insurance, Inspections, and Homeowners Insurance

Homeownership is a big decision because you are making a major purchase and providing security for your family that will last for years and for generations to come. This process is not one to take lightly. With any important decision, there are risks involved, so you want to minimize the effects of those risks. And, buying a home is no different. I want you to take steps to protect your precious investment, your home.

Title Insurance

Title insurance is insurance that ensures that you are the rightful owner of the property when you purchase it. It protects you against other people claiming that they own your property. When you have title insurance, a title search is performed by the title company to ensure that no one else has claim to your property. Of course, there is a possibility that someone may have a claim to your property. However, having title insurance reduces the likelihood of that happening. When purchasing title insurance, be sure to get owner's title insurance, which protects you against claims on your property.[7] Having to give your property to another person because she has ownership rights to the property that you thought was purchased legitimately is not a good experience, so get title insurance to prevent such an event.

Inspections

Before closing the deal on your new home, you should have your house inspected for problems that may be wrong with the house. Is the house structurally sound? Does it have mold? Are there electrical issues that could cause a fire? What is the actual value of the home, and how does the value compare to other homes in the area and similar homes that have sold in the same area? Has the land been surveyed to ensure that the acreage is accurate? All of these questions can be answered by seeking a professional to perform inspections, appraisals, and land surveys to give you piece of mind about the house you plan to buy.

- *Contractor*: If you are buying a house that is already built, make sure to meet with the developer or contractor to see if the house is structurally sound. Was the home built with quality products, or was it built with cheap materials that did not meet quality standards? Some houses may be hard to resell due to how they were designed. People may not want to pay for a house that looks "ugly." The location may be ideal, but if the house is poorly designed, buyers may frown on making you an offer when you want to sell.

- *Mold and Radon Inspector*: Mold or radon in your home can cause health problems if left unchecked. Have a professional restoration service search for signs of mold or radon in the house before you commit to buying.

- *Electrical*: Faulty electrical wiring is a major concern in a house. If the house you are purchasing has wiring issues, the wiring could put your family at danger of an electrical fire. I highly recommend having a professional electrician inspect the electrical wiring throughout the house to ensure that it is properly wired.

- *Land Survey*: Has the property been surveyed recently to make sure that you are paying the correct amount for land value? Are the property lines accurate, so you know where the property begins and ends? By having the property surveyed, both of those questions will be answered. You will have an accurate acreage of the house and where the boundaries are on your property via a land survey.

- *Appraisal*: How much is the house really worth? How does the price of the house compare to other houses in the area? An appraisal will definitely answer those questions for you. An appraisal is just a professional's opinion of the value of a house. I suggest getting at last two or three comparisons of value to make sure that you are getting a fair value of the home.

Homeowners Insurance

What do you do when you buy something of significant value? You would probably consider insuring the item against loss, right? Well, a home purchase is surely a purchase that requires protecting from loss. Just like car insurance, homeowners insurance provides protection against loss in the event of a catastrophic event. I recommend getting a homeowner's policy that will replace the full value of your home if an unexpected event occurs and causes you to lose your home. Let me illustrate like this.

You buy your first home that is worth $140,000 and get that amount of coverage through your homeowner's insurance policy. Over time, your home's value increases to $170,000. However, you forget to update the policy to cover the additional $30,000 increase. If your home were to get destroyed by a fire or tornado, you would only receive $140,000 from your insurance company instead of the $170,000. When your home's value increases, you want to ensure that your insurance company offers full replacement cost, which would cover the entire amount of loss (i.e., up to the $170,000 value in the example).

I also recommend reviewing your homeowner's insurance policy annually and updating it as needed to make sure your insurance coverage is adequate for you and your family.

The Most Important Thing: LOCATION!

In real estate, the most important thing is location, location, location! The location of any property is pivotal in determining its value. If you are looking for a house to buy in a great area of town, you will likely pay more for the house than you would for the same house in a low-income area. However, you could put a house that is not in excellent condition in an upscale area of a city and probably double the value of the house just based on the location. Be sure to search for a house that is in an area that has the potential to increase the value of the property.

In addition to the property's location, having a house close to water increases the property's value. There's something about water that creates a sense of serenity and tranquility leading people to a relaxed mood. Water has that "wow" factor. People pay more money for that "wow" factor. Research shows that buyers pay more for waterfront properties, for valid reasons. Some reasons that people pay more for houses near water, whether an ocean, lake, or river, are desirability, the view, the tranquility, and the privacy. There's also an entire lifestyle that comes with living on the water. For people that boat, swim, sunbathe, or paddle board, living on the water gives you access to your favorite activities anytime the weather permits.[8]

Another factor increasing the value of a waterfront property is scarcity. In fact, land for development of waterfront properties is scarce, and when something is scarce, the value increases. If there is high demand and little supply, the price for an item is high. High demand plus low supply equals high cost.[9]

Hendersonville, Tennessee is a great example of a city on a lake. The city's lake, Old Hickory Lake, creates a real "view" for its waterfront homeowners. Sometimes after attending church on Sunday, Shameka and I go to the lake to experience the beauty and wonder of God's creation. It's a no-brainer the reason that people pay more for waterfront homes.

Manual Underwriting: No Score Loans

Let's face it. We live in a world that revolves around using borrowed money. When I traveled as an auditor, I worked for a company that bought bad debt. The company purchased bad, or charged offed, debt that meant that people did not pay, and the owner of the debt did not collect it. The debt owner sold it to my employer. Heck, I even used a credit card to travel! It is kind of weird to work for a company that makes profit from people not paying their credit card bills, and I was using the same vice! I knew what could happen to me if I did not pay my credit card bill, I would be on the other side having a bill collector call me to collect the debt.

The American culture thrives on using credit. The credit score, or FICO Score, created by the Fair Isaac Corporation is a measurement of one's credit worthiness or riskiness. When you apply for a credit card, car loan, or mortgage, lenders want to know if you will repay the loan. Lenders request a copy of your credit report and FICO Score to determine how likely you are to repay the debt. The FICO Score shows how often you have interacted with debt. In fact, the FICO Score indicates how much you have used debt; it does not measure how much money you saved, invested, given, or your level of wealth. Despite those shortcomings, the FICO Score is widely used to measure people's credit worthiness (or lack thereof). Here is how the FICO Score is calculated:

- Payment history: 35%
- Amounts owed: 30%
- Length of credit history: 15%
- Credit mix in use (credit cards, mortgage loans, retail accounts): 10%
- New credit: 10%.[10]

Do you see a pattern? I do. The FICO Score is a measure of how much people love debt. All of those line items indicate debt usage. If you have a high FICO Score of 800 or higher, it says, "I REALLY LOVE

DEBT!" Banks also use credit scores to determine someone's credit worthiness.

Do you need a FICO Score to get a home loan? No. You do not need a FICO Score to get approved for a mortgage. If you do not have a credit score because you have not borrowed money, you still can get a home loan by doing manual underwriting. Underwriting is simply when a lender receives payment from a borrower in exchange for accepting potential risk.[11] In the case of a mortgage, a bank would receive interest payments (when you pay your monthly payment) in return accepts the risk of you potentially not paying the loan. Manual underwriting is when a lender requests information about your payment history such as housing payments such as rent, utilities (electricity, gas, water, and Internet service providers), and school tuition to identify your credit worthiness; those payments would be called "non-traditional credit sources."[12] Traditional credit is having a FICO Score. In addition to reviewing the non-traditional credit elements, the lender would also request your current income, current debt level, and other financial documents. A manual underwriting loan requires more documentation and a little more time because additional credit documentation need to be reviewed by an underwriter, according to Churchill Mortgage Corporation.[13] Anything worth doing takes time; the manual underwriting process is no different.

I want to pause for a moment to congratulate you for staying with me on this journey. Talking about buying a house with cash or getting a fifteen year, fixed-rate mortgage is countercultural, so the odds are stacked against me. I want you to stand out from the crowd. I know people that have purchased homes with a thirty-year mortgage, which means the borrower has a lower monthly payment. However, over the long term, the borrower pays more interest for a thirty year, fixed-rate mortgage in comparison to a fifteen year, fixed-rate mortgage. I recommend getting rid of the mortgage debt as soon as possible. Want to pay off your home mortgage? Let me show you how!

Mortgage Crushing

At this point, you have increased your $500 - $1,500 Rainy Day Fund to three to nine months of living expenses, paid off all of your consumer debt, are investing 10% to 15% of your household earnings into stock mutual funds and tax favored retirement plans, and saving for your children's college education. Now it's time to press the accelerator on your wealth accumulation plan! In addition to funding your retirement and children's college education, I recommend crushing the mortgage debt as fast as you can!

In order to crush the mortgage debt, you need to exert some emotional and physical energy! To crush your mortgage debt, you must be

FOCUSED, FIERCE, and ON FIRE! There is no other way to destroy the house debt unless you are focused, fierce, and on fire. By being lackluster with getting out of debt keeps you in debt longer. I do not want you to remain in debt longer than you have to. I want you to hate debt! Why? Remember: Debt is a thief that comes to steal, kill, and destroy your dreams, hopes, and desires.

I recommend working overtime at your job, increasing sales in your business, getting a part-time job, or being creative to increase your income to accelerate the mortgage crushing process. If you have a thirty year, fixed-rate mortgage I encourage you to pay it off in fifteen years. Or, if you have a fifteen year, fixed-rate mortgage I urge you to pay the mortgage off in seven to ten years. You may be able to refinance your mortgage from a thirty-year, fixed rate to a fifteen year, fixed-rate mortgage. Refinancing is when a borrower requests of the lender to change the loan term (i.e., length of loan period), interest rate change, or to change the mortgage payment (temporarily). Essentially, the borrower is applying for another loan.

Can you dream with me for a moment? Imagine if you had no car payment, student loan payment, credit card payment, or mortgage payment? What could you do for your family? How could you impact your community? How could you help people around the world? Visualize how you would feel; taste the emotion when you make your final mortgage payment. Wow! Does it feel great! I want to help you become debt free and accumulate wealth to be able to enrich other peoples' lives.

In addition, think about how much money you could save if you did not have a mortgage payment. Instead of sending money to a bank each month, you could put that money in your retirement account. Over time, you will accumulate so much wealth that you will be able to do whatever you want to do. Quit your job, start a business, volunteer, travel the world, spend time with you family and friends; the possibilities are endless. I will discuss wealth later in this book. But for now, know that you will be able to accumulate wealth if you are debt free. I want you to get there. You can do it...if you decide to do it!

Going Once, Going Twice, Sold!

Do you remember when you bought your first car? I do. I wanted a car, so I worked to save money to buy my first car. As a high school teenager, I worked a part-time job at a local car wash to save money. I found a car in a different city than I lived. I saved about $1,000, and my dad took me to look at the car. It was a 1986 Oldsmobile Cutlass Supreme with gray interior seats and exterior paint. The car was well maintained and clean.

My dad and I test drove the car, and I was pleased with the performance, so I bought it. I was filled with excitement and ready to take my new ride the distance! What did the seller do to persuade me to make the purchase? He made sure that the car's appearance appealed to my liking by cleaning it. The car also had a fair price. Whether you are selling lemonade, hair products, or a jar of peanut butter, you must be able to persuade consumers to exchange their money for your product or service.

Not only is buying a home a big decision to make, selling a home is a major decision as well. Selling a home takes great persuasion because people will be trading a large sum of money for a big asset. Making sure that your home is ready to sell is paramount. We will discuss some important tips to help you sell your home and get the price that you desire.

Show Me The Bling

Once I was in Atlanta, GA visiting one of my cousins, Valerie. I went to a shopping mall to do some "window shopping." As I walked through one department store, I looked at the clothes on the racks and was disappointed in what I saw. Although the clothes were "new" and ready to sell, the clothes appeared worn. What made the clothes look used and worn? The store's lighting. The lighting was dim, which made the clothes look dark and used. Then, another time I visited a shopping mall in the Buckhead area of Atlanta. I went to a department store, and the clothes' appearance outshined the clothes of the other shopping mall. The reason: The lighting. The lighting at the Buckhead shopping mall was bright and welcoming compared to the other shopping mall with its dim, uninviting lighting.

When selling your house, the lighting matters as well. I recommend putting new light bulbs in every room to increase the lighting throughout the house. We want the prospective home buyer to feel welcome and to have the interior of the house attract the customer.

Another simple tip that you could implement is cleaning your windows, especially the glass in your front door. If the prospective customer comes to the front door to tour the house and sees children's finger prints or pet prints on the glass, he may request a lower price for the house or worse, not purchase. Those little nuances can cause the house not to sell, so make sure you clean the windows and glass doors thoroughly with some glass cleaner.

Imagine being the prospective customer waiting outside the front door of the house to tour before making an offer to buy. As you wait, you look up and see cob webs, spiders, and dead insects dangling above your head. Yikes! How would that experience make you feel about the house? Therefore, as the seller I recommend putting yourself in the buyer's shoes and understand the buyer's perspective. I would clean those spiders, insects, and cob webs immediately before the prospective customer arrives. Another great selling tip is to create an environment that gets the attention of the buyer's sense of smell. When you go to a bakery, the smell of fresh baked bread, cookies, cakes, and other delicious food make your mouth water and entice you to buy. I recommend tickling the buyer's sense of smell by baking bread or cookies in the house before the prospect arrives. By doing this, you will establish an inviting environment for the prospective customer and likely stimulate her thoughts of baking in her "new home" creating memories with her family. If you are not a baker, another idea would be to put some vanilla extract in the oven and turn it on to spread the aroma throughout the house.

This last tip should be obvious, but I think it is worth mentioning. Be sure that your lawn and surrounding plants, trees, and shrubs are properly maintained. Imagine that you are buying a house and when you arrive to view it, the lawn is as tall as jack in the bean stalk. I mean, that grass is so tall that it would take a week to get it cut! Not to mention any unwanted friends (i.e., snakes) that may find a home in the yard. Ultimately, the unmanaged lawn would cause you not to buy the house and would warrant you to move to the next house for sale.

Don't let this happen to you. Instead, I want you to create a "wow" factor for the prospective buyer by developing what is called "curb appeal." Curb appeal is that "wow" factor, meaning the house attracts someone's attention when viewed from the curb. The house's appearance is enhanced when the lawn is immaculate and neatly cut and edged to perfection. I recommend having a fresh cut lawn, sidewalks edged, weeds removed, and scrubs and bushes manicured to entice the prospective buyer to want to see what's behind the four walls of her new home. If you can hire a professional landscaping company to provide a picture-perfect view, I suggest doing so.

Once you have taken the steps to attract buyers to your home, the next thing to do is take pictures of it and put them on the Internet. For 43% of recent buyers, the first step that they took in the home buying process was to look online at properties for sale.[14] If people are using the Internet to search for homes, it is important to provide quality information to the prospective buyers. Therefore, I suggest taking high-quality photographs of your house and uploading them to the Internet. You are selling your most valuable asset, so you want to make a great first impression. By having professional grade photos of your home posted online you will likely get many prospective customer views of your photos, with the expectation of making a sale.

Stay Away From Do-It-Yourself
When it comes to selling your home, attempting to do it yourself will cause you to lose lots of money and add more stress to your life. Some

people may not want to pay a real estate agent a commission to sell their home. However, a high-quality professional real estate agent will get you the best price for your home. Selling your home yourself may be cheaper in the short-term, but in the long-term, having a professional do the heavy lifting for you will make your life much easier. Research shows that 89% of sellers used a real estate agent to sell their home.[15] Why? First, real estate agents sell houses for a living; the average person does not, unless he is a real estate agent. Real estate agents are knowledgeable about the sales process and the real estate market. They are the experts. Second, real estate agents sell houses at a higher price than sellers that sell their own home. According to research, homes sold by For-Sale-by-Owner (FSBO) sellers typically sell for less than the selling price of other homes and significantly lower than agent-assisted homes.[16]

When searching for a real estate agent, you want to get a high-quality, professional real estate agent with integrity and knows how to sell homes. I suggest not hiring a friend or relative to work with you. I recommend finding a real estate agent that has experience selling homes for at least five years, has integrity, sells an average of one hundred houses each year, and most importantly, has a heart to serve and teach customers. In addition, I recommend interviewing at least three or four real estate agents to make sure he is a great fit to work on your behalf. Have the real estate agent give you a presentation, so you can see him in action and get an idea of how he will present when selling your home. I encourage you to ask plenty of questions when interviewing prospective real estate agents. He should have your best interest in mind, willing to serve you to make you feel comfortable during the sales process. If you do not feel comfortable or do not get a good "vibe" from him, continue looking for the best real estate agent to meet your needs. I recommend getting a professional to help you sell your home.

Action Steps to Maximize Your Money to Stop Being Broke
1. Decide to pay cash for a house or to get a fifteen year, fixed-rate mortgage with a monthly payment no bigger than 25% of your take-home earnings with a 10% or 20% down payment.
2. Pay off your home mortgage as fast as you can! Get focused, fierce, and on fire!
3. Find a professional real estate agent that has your best interest in mind when buying and selling a home.

9
Simplifying Insurance: A Shield of Protection
Protecting Your Family, Income, and Legacy

I want to congratulate you on staying with me on this journey to not be broke! It has been a challenging journey; in fact, that may be an understatement! It has been very, very difficult to make it this far! Why? Because change is hard; we do not like change. The change that you have experienced thus far will reap benefits for generations to come.

So far, we have discussed saving for unexpected events, creating a monthly budget, destroying debt, investing for retirement, saving for your children's college education, and eliminating mortgage debt. That's a lot of information to process. By this point you may be saving $1,500 for your mini Rainy Day Fund. Or, you may be paying off credit card debt, student loans, and car loans. Wherever you are on this journey, I congratulate you and urge you to keep moving forward!

Now, I want you to imagine that you have nothing in savings for your Rainy Day Fund, you have $10,000 of credit card debt, and have a $150,000 mortgage. One autumn morning you are getting your children ready for school. The usual morning routine occurs as your children scurry to get ready for the commute. You finish packing lunches and loading everyone into the car and off you go to transport the children to school.

As you are driving, a van suddenly cuts in front of you, and then stops at the stop light causing you to slam on the brakes. You barely miss hitting the van. However, the car behind you plows into you from behind creating a domino effect. The van you tried to avoid hitting is now totally damaged because the momentum from the car behind forced your car into the rear of the van. Bummer! At that moment you think, "Do we have enough car insurance coverage? Will we be able to pay the other party's medical bills? What if this accident bankrupts us? How will we fix our car?"

In a time of crisis as described above, not having a Rainy Day Fund and having debt adds fuel to the fire because you are not prepared for life's unexpected events. However, by having a Rainy Day Fund and being debt free, there is another shield of protection available to reduce risk in your life: Insurance.

In this chapter, we will discuss insurance, the importance of having it, the types of insurance available, and other related topics. I want to highlight the necessity of insurance and its role in moving toward not being broke.

Insurance: A Necessary Tool for Your Financial Plan

Insurance is an important part of a healthy financial plan. It helps you protect the assets that you own such as houses, cars, and your income. What is insurance? Insurance is protection that you buy to transfer risk from you to another entity. For example, when you buy car insurance you are transferring the risk of replacing someone's car or paying her medical bills, in an event of an accident, to an insurance company. The insurance company accepts most of the risk in return for the payment, or premium, that you pay for insurance coverage. The insurance company agrees to take a majority of the risk, you take some risk, and in exchange, you pay the insurance company. That is basically how insurance works. Since insurance companies have more money than you and me, they can handle paying for the "big" risks. Therefore, we can pay for the "little" risks with the Rainy Day Fund. That is the reason for having both insurance and a Rainy Day Fund because they reduce the risk in our lives.

There are many types of insurance available for protection. Specially, I want to discuss the type of insurance that I recommend getting for a healthy financial plan. Here is the list.

- Auto Insurance
- Homeowner's (or Renter's) Insurance
- Health Insurance
- Term Life Insurance
- Long Term Disability Insurance
- Long Term Care Insurance
- Identity Theft Protection

Let's discuss each type of coverage.

Auto Insurance

When I was in elementary school, two of my siblings and I were on a school bus riding home from school. I may have been in fourth or fifth grade at the time, so I was about ten or eleven years old. It was an ordinary day of just riding the bus home to do homework and play outside with the other neighborhood children, or so I thought. When the bus stopped, suddenly someone rear ended us. We were not hurt terribly. Afterward, my siblings and I went to a chiropractor for body adjustments to correct the physical ailments caused by the bus accident. We probably went to the chiropractor for several weeks. We did not have to pay for the chiropractor appointments. Why? Because the person that hit the bus had insurance, and the insurance paid for the medical bills. Eventually, a lawyer working on our behalf was able to award my siblings and me money for the bus accident. Luckily for us, we did not have to go to court; that would have been a grown-up responsibility, and we were not ready for that.

That is an example of how auto insurance works. You pay a premium to an insurance company (i.e., transferring risk) to cover some of the costs if an auto accident occurs. The amount of risk you take is in the form of the deductible. A deductible is the amount you pay, in addition to the premium, before the insurance company covers the remaining amount of damages due to an accident. Say you have a $1,000 deductible, and you have an accident. You would need to pay the $1,000 before your insurance paid the remaining damages and costs that are above the $1,000. In addition, insurance coverage is quoted in this format: $100,000/$300,000/$100,000.

The first amount, $100,000, represents the maximum amount that would be paid to cover bodily injuries for each person (other party) involved in the accident. The second amount, $300,000, is the maximum amount for bodily injuries the insurance company would pay per accident; and the last number, $100,000, is the limit the insurance company will pay for property damage to the other party's property per accident. This type of insurance is usually liability cover, which means it only covers damages for the other party's bodily injuries and property. If you want to have your insurance pay for your damages, you would need to purchase collision coverage.

If you had liability insurance with 100/300/100 coverage, and you have an accident that causes bodily injuries of $80,000 and $50,000 in property damages. You would have enough insurance to pay for the bodily injuries and property damages. However, if three people each had bodily injuries of $120,000 and the property damage amounted to $110,000, then you would not have enough coverage. Why? Because the total bodily injury amount would be $360,000, which exceeds the $300,000 maximum limit for bodily injury coverage for each accident; and the $110,000 for property damage is more than your $100,000 coverage. Therefore, you would need to pay $70,000 out of pocket for the difference. Ouch! The other party could sue you to pay for the remaining damages, so make sure you have the right amount of coverage. I suggest at least a 100/300/100 policy as a minimum; get more coverage if you can afford it.

Homeowner's and Renter's Insurance

Buying a home is an exciting experience! You have worked hard to get out of debt and save a down payment for the house. It is only right that you work hard to keep your home as well. We discussed the specifics of homeowner's insurance in the last chapter. Make sure to review it again for a refresher on homeowner's insurance.

If you are still renting a home or apartment, renter's insurance is the type of insurance you need to cover your belongings as a renter. Renter's insurance provides coverage for the contents in the apartment or home. Some rental apartment homes require you to buy renter's insurance while you are a resident. If your contents are damaged due to a fire, for example, the insurance company will pay to replace the damaged items up to the coverage amount that you purchase. Here is a suggestion: Record all of the contents in your home with a video camera, estimate the value of the contents, and get coverage equal to or greater than the value of your items.

Health Insurance

Health insurance has been a hot topic of discussion since Obamacare required all U.S. Americans to have health insurance. Now that a new president of the U.S. has been inaugurated, a fight to reverse Obamacare is at hand. Stay tuned for the results. While the war on health insurance continues, I want you to be armed with health coverage whether or not the U.S. government requires it because protecting your family is a priority. According to one source, a vast number of people are influenced by medical expenses to file for bankruptcy in America.[1] Having health insurance is a necessity to protect you and your family.

Let's talk about the specifics of health insurance. First, we need to define some terms that are common with health insurance. Just like auto insurance, health insurance also has a deductible. You may also have to pay a co-payment, which is a set amount you pay each time you visit a doctor, specialist, or emergency room. Shameka and I have a co-payment whenever we visit the doctor, and we pay a co-payment if we visit a specialist. If your employer does not pay for 100% of your health coverage, then you might have coinsurance.

Coinsurance is the shared percentage that you and your insurance company pay regarding medical bills. Your coinsurance may be 80/20 or 70/30. For example, you may have coinsurance of 80/20, which means that any medical expense that hits the deductible, such as an MRI, would be covered at 80% by the insurance company and you would pay 20% of the bill once you reach your deductible. If you had a $1,000 medical expense, you would pay $200; the insurance company would pay $800. When Shameka and I had our daughter, Naomi, we paid our percentage of the remaining balance of coinsurance.

In addition, you may have an out-of-pocket maximum amount that you pay. The out-of-pocket maximum is the total amount that you would pay for medical bills, including the deductible and coinsurance.

Once you meet that "magic number," the insurance company pays 100% of your medical expenses. Pretty sweet deal! Another number that may be of interest to you is the maximum lifetime limit. With the maximum lifetime limit, your insurance company would pay up to a certain limit and afterward stop paying for medical expenses. This number is normally about $2,000,000, so unless you have chronic health problems you may never reach this amount in medical expenses.

Here is a money savings tip for insurance: To lower your monthly insurance premium, raise your deductible to an amount that you can afford (i.e., let your Rainy Day Fund be the measuring stick). By raising your deductible, you accept more risk financially. Let me give an illustration. If your deductible is $250, and you increase it to $1,000, that means you are accepting $750 more risk. The cost savings is $75 to increase the deductible. How long will it take you to recover your cost? It would take you ten years to recover your cost (i.e., $750/$75 = 10 years). You have to decide whether the savings is worth the time to recover the cost.

Another option to save money on your medical costs is to get a Health Savings Account (HSA). An HSA is a tax-exempt (i.e., not taxed) savings account that is used to pay certain medical expenses. To qualify for an HSA, you must have a high deductible health plan (HDHP), which is health coverage that has a usually high deductible (e.g., $5,000 or higher). There are several benefits for having an HSA in addition to being tax exempt that include 1) contributions to an HSA are deductible on your Federal income tax return, 2) contributions through your employer reduce your taxable income, 3) the money stays in the account until you use it, and 4) the money in the account grows tax free! As icing on the cake, once you meet your high deductible, the insurance company pays 100% of your medical costs! Is that a sweet deal or what? If you qualify and can afford it, I recommend getting an HSA.

An HSA works best when you are very healthy and when you are unhealthy. Here's why. When you are healthy, you will hardly use the HSA for major medical expenses because you maintain a healthy lifestyle. And when you go to the doctor, you have the money saved in the HSA to cover the costs. In addition, since you do not go to the doctor that often, you will have a big stash of cash accumulating each year as you put money in the HSA for medical expenses. Secondly, if you have really bad illnesses or have a lot of medical issues, then you will probably meet your high deductible pretty quickly. As you go to the doctor, you will be paying the medical bills, which will go toward your deductible. Once the deductible is met, your insurance company will pay 100% of the remaining medical bills.

Term Life Insurance

Recently my siblings, parents, and I did a Skype session over the telephone. The primary topics discussed were my parents' final requests regarding death and life insurance. We had to be responsible adults and talk about topics that many people probably avoid. Discussing death may evoke feelings of sadness and sorrow of losing a loved one. However, openly talking about death and making plans to address it prepares you in advance, which means that you are being proactive instead of reactive. Being reactive will add stress to your life in a time when you are mourning. We were able to talk about my parent's wishes about burial, funeral arrangements, and life insurance policies. Let's discuss life insurance. What is it? How does it work? Why do you need it?

Life insurance is insurance that provides money to your beneficiaries (i.e., people that you want to receive the funds), when you die. Technically it is "death insurance." The money provided replaces your income. It allows your family to continue to have income as if you were still living and working at your job or in your business. How does it work? With a life insurance policy in place, at your death, your spouse or beneficiary receives the death benefits. Once he receives the money, the beneficiary would talk to a professional investment advisor to invest the money in stock mutual funds that earn at least a 10% rate of return. Then, the beneficiary withdraws 10% each year of the gross benefit amount as income. Here's an example.

Donna and Chip have an annual income of $50,000 and each has a twenty-year $500,000 term life insurance policy. Unfortunately, Chip unexpectedly passes away. Donna would receive $500,000 at her husband's death; thereafter, Donna would invest the money in mutual funds with a 10% rate of return. And each year she would withdraw $50,000 to use for living expenses. Donna just replaced Chip's income by having term life insurance. How much stress would this relieve from your life during a time of loss by having term life insurance? Shameka and I both have life insurance, so we are being proactive instead of reactive; I encourage you to do the same. I suggest getting a term life insurance policy that is ten to twelve times your annual income. Not all life insurance is beneficial to the insured. I recommend only buying term life insurance because it is just simple insurance as explained above. It is also less expensive than other types of life insurance such as whole life, universal life insurance, and variable life insurance. Let's discuss the specifics of each type.

Whole Life Insurance

Whole, or permanent, life insurance is life insurance that insures you for the rest of your life; hence, "whole" life. Whole life insurance also has a savings account, or cash value, part of the policy, which makes it more expensive than term life insurance. As you pay your premium, a portion of it goes into cash value. However, when you pass away, the beneficiaries only get the face amount of the policy. For instance, if your spouse has a $100,000 whole life insurance policy that built up a $25,000 cash value, and she dies. You would receive $125,000 from the insurance company, right? Wrong. You would only receive the face value of the policy, $100,000. The insurance company keeps the cash value of $25,000.

In addition, the cash value has a low rate of return. According to research, the average annual rate of return for whole life insurance with cash value is 3.5%.[2] If you buy whole life insurance with cash value, it is like mixing insurance and investing. I recommend keeping insurance and investing separate. I also recommend buying term life insurance and investing the difference between the cost of term life insurance and whole life insurance. The bottom line: Stay away from whole life insurance!

Universal Life Insurance
Universal life insurance is a variation of whole life insurance. It also has a cash value feature. However, with universal life insurance, the policy holder can change the premium and death benefits of the policy.[3] Additional features may have been included to make the product attractive to consumers. Universal life insurance is similar to whole life insurance, so I recommend not buying this type of insurance.

Variable Life Insurance
Variable life insurance is a product with features a step above universal life insurance. Variable life insurance is a permanent life insurance product with separate accounts comprised of various instruments and investment funds such as stocks, bonds, equity funds, money market funds, and bond funds.[4] Variable life insurance is another insurance product that combines insurance and investing, so I suggest running away from this product if an insurance agent tries to sell it to you.

The lesson that I want to teach you about life insurance is to only buy term life insurance. It is not expensive compared to the alternatives, and it provides coverage that will allow your family to continue to have its needs met when you are no longer living. Buying term life insurance lets your family know that you care about them even in your absence.

Long Term Disability Insurance
One of my cousins worked at a major tire manufacturer that also made building products. My cousin, Roger (his name has been changed to protect his identity), operated a forklift for his job. I was talking to him a while ago about an injury he suffered while working. One day he was

driving a forklift down an incline in a warehouse, and as the forklift came down the incline it injured my cousin's back by landing awkwardly. Eventually, my cousin had back surgery to correct the problem. What would you do if you suffered a devastating injury like my cousin? How would you be able to pay your bills?

Here's another story about someone that I know that experienced a disability. This lady, let's call her Sue, is a superwoman. In fact, she has more than five children and several grandchildren. As a young mother, she worked at dry cleaners and cleaned houses to make ends meet. She and her husband both worked to provide for their family. Sue eventually started working at a movie theater selling food at the concession stands. As Sue grew older, she experienced problems with her legs that ultimately forced her to become disabled. Now, she gets disability income from the Federal government. What if you became disabled? How would you meet your basis needs? These are tough questions to answer, yet, thought provoking.

Research shows that 25% of twenty-year olds will become disabled before retirement age.[5] So young people can become disabled as well. Two primary causes of disability are related to 1) back, muscle, and joint injuries, and 2) cancer. Disability can happen to anyone, just like it happened to Roger and Sue. However, you can be prepared if it happens to you or a loved one. Here's how.

With disability insurance, you want to purchase long-term disability insurance not short-term disability. Remember: The mega Rainy Day Fund of three to nine months of living expenses will cover the "small" risks. Let the insurance companies handle the "large" risks such as long-term disability due to injury. I recommend getting long term disability insurance that provides coverage over a long period of time; for at least one year or longer. I purchased long term disability insurance for myself that will last until I am age 65. Disability insurance has a waiting period called the elimination period that is similar to a deductible. The elimination period is the time you must wait before you receive disability payments. The longer the elimination period the lower your insurance premium will be. An elimination period could be 30, 60, 90, or 180 days. I recommend selecting an elimination period equal to the number of months you have saved in your Rainy Day Fund.

When you purchase long-term disability insurance, you want to make sure to get coverage that will provide at least 60% of your current income level. This means that if you become disabled, the insurance company will pay you 60% of your current income level. Let me illustrate. Suppose you earn $70,000 a year, have a five-year disability insurance policy with a 60-day elimination period, and you become disabled due to a back injury. After the elimination period has passed the insurance company will pay you $42,000 ($70,000 * .60 = $42,000) for five years. In addition, you want to make sure that the policy provides "Own Occupation" coverage. Own occupation, or "Own Occ," is disability insurance coverage that will pay benefits if you become disabled and cannot perform the job that you were formally trained to do. If you went to school for accounting, and your disability does not allow you to do accounting, then the insurance company will pay you disability benefits. However, with Own Occ, it only pays for a certain amount of time. I suggest having a backup plan to make a career change to do something that you can do even if you are temporarily disabled.

If you can get long-term disability insurance through an association that you are affiliated with, I suggest getting it because you will probably be able to buy it for a really low rate compared to the open market.

Long Term Care Insurance

When my grandfather passed away in the late 1990s, he left behind my grandmother. My grandmother lived at home, but eventually had to be admitted into a nursing home. The nursing home was not the best regarding quality of service. In fact, there was a time when a caregiver gave my grandmother too much insulin; my grandmother was a diabetic. Had she been in a nursing home that provided quality service, this issue could have been prevented. Because my grandparents did not have proper insurance, my grandmother had to settle for a low-quality nursing home facility. I want you and your family to be ready in the event that one of your family members needs assisted living.

I recommend talking with your parents about getting long term care insurance once they become age 60. Long term care insurance provides insurance to help with assisted living, nursing home, or home care expenses. Caring for an aging parent living in a nursing home can be expensive. If your parents have assets such as a home or investments, assisted living expenses can put a strain on those assets, especially if they do not have long term care insurance. For example, if your father is not healthy and uses $300,000 of investments for his medical expenses; then, he dies leaving your mother with $100,000 of investments. Later, she goes into an assisted living facility for five to ten years (that's about how long my grandmother stayed in a nursing home). That $100,000 will probably be used in one year, leaving her with no money to pay for the nursing home expenses. Ouch.

Why should you get long term care insurance when you become age 60? Research shows that you are less likely to file a claim before age 70. About 96% of claims are filed for people age 70 and older.[6] The cost of buying long term care insurance may be cheaper if you bought it before age 60, say at age 50, but you would likely not file a claim for the next ten years. Instead of buying long term care insurance, I suggest investing the money you would spend and put it into mutual funds until you reach age 60.

Lastly, if you have parents that are approaching age 60, I encourage you to talk to them about buying long term care insurance. This one discussion could have a major impact in helping you care for your parents as they age.

Identity Theft Protection

As an accountant, I worked for a certified public accountant in a city outside of Nashville, Tennessee. We prepared Federal income tax returns for clients, and one day I heard my boss talking to a client that had her identity stolen. The client had to contact the Internal Revenue Service to get a certain number or code to allow her to get her tax return filed. She probably spent hours resolving the issue. What is identity theft?

Identity theft is when someone steals your personal or financial information such as your name, address, Social Security number, or bank information to use it for their personal gain; for example, they may use your information to open credit card accounts. It is difficult to prevent identity theft because our personal information is everywhere! Think about all of the places that require you to give them your personal information: Doctors and dentists for medical and dental appointments; banks and credit unions when opening accounts or getting a loan; and insurance companies for getting insurance policies. Places of business also have people's personal information on file. Becoming a victim of identity theft can happen to anyone.

Identity theft affects about one in twenty Americans each year. According to Javelin's 2020 Identity Fraud Survey, 13 million consumers in the U.S. were affected by identity fraud in 2019 with total fraud losses of nearly $17 billion.[7] That is a lot of money! Identity theft is a big deal in America! Thieves can steal your information by going through your trash, stealing your mail from your mailbox, or steal it from your computer. There are ways to safeguard your personal information. Here are a few ways:

- Shred your personal documents such as bank statements, medical bills, and junk mail; use a cross-cut shredder to destroy your documents
- Password protect your electronic devices such as cell phones, computers, and tablets; make your passwords at least eight digits long using a mixture of upper and lowercase letters, numbers, and special characters

- Keep your debit card in a cardholder, and make sure that you put it back in its place after each use; if possible, use cash when dining out to prevent loss or theft
- Do not put documents with your personal information in your trash can or dumpster; thieves may go through your documents to steal it (known as dumpster diving)
- Get a free credit report to check your credit for suspicious activity; get a free credit report every four months from one of the credit reporting agencies (Experian, Equifax, and Trans Union).

Some companies may offer credit monitoring services, which means that a company monitors your credit activity and alerts you when suspicious activity occurs. Credit monitoring does not prevent your identity from being stolen. There is another way to protect yourself from becoming a victim. I recommend getting identity theft protection that assigns an associate to work on your behalf to resolve the problem if your identity is stolen. According to research, the average time it takes to fix an identity theft issue is seven hours, usually over the course of a day (most common) up to a month. In extreme cases, people may spend 1,200 hours over the course of a year or more resolving identity theft problems.[8] So if you have someone else handling your identity theft case, you can continue to be productive at work instead of being on the phone trying to resolve the issue yourself.

In addition to identity theft, be aware of IRS scams. If someone calls you and tells you that he works for the IRS and demands money from you, hang up the phone! The IRS will not call you; the IRS will contact you by sending you a letter in the mail, never by phone.

Final Word on Insurance

Having insurance is a major part of a sound financial plan. You are on a path to maximize your money to stop being broke, and as you travel along you want to make sure you are protecting your family, your assets, and yourself. I want you to be prepared when life's challenges happen to you. Having a good defense will help you keep the things that you have worked hard to earn. Make sure you get the proper insurance in all of the areas that we have discussed.

Action Steps to Maximize Your Money to Stop Being Broke

1. Meet with your spouse or accountability partner and review your current insurance policies.
2. Make a list of the types of insurance that you need to purchase.
3. Contact an insurance professional (with a caring heart, has your best interest in mind, and is willing to teach you more about insurance) to discuss the insurance options highlighted in this chapter.

4. Purchase the necessary insurance policies to protect you and your family.

   Remember: First, understand; then, buy the insurance.

Surplus, Anyone?
Wealth Accumulation

As I mentioned in the foreword of this book, I grew up in a low-income family. My family received government assistance in the form of food stamps and WIC (women, infants, and children). Despite being on welfare, my parents worked to provide us the necessities and some luxuries. I enjoyed when other neighborhood children came to play video games with my siblings and me. I had a blast spending time with my family and friends at the park. I remember a time when my mother had a birthday party for one of my siblings. We had cake and ice cream and many of our friends came to enjoy the festivities! We did not have a lot of money, but we had each other. Sure, we had the latest video game console, but we also had love for one another. We were content.

Contentment is something that I personally have struggled with because I am very ambitious and have big dreams. However, I want those dreams to happen now rather than later. As we have learned thus far that moving toward not being broke is a journey and a process. Scripture talks about being content; "So if we have enough food and clothing, let us be content."[1] I am learning that you can be content and still be focused on achieving a goal. The apostle Paul talked about being content in the book of Timothy; he also was pressing forward *while* being content at the same time. Paul had a "forward focused" mindset and contentment simultaneously. Paul said, "I focus on this one thing: Forgetting the past and looking forward to what lies ahead, I press on to reach the end of the race and receive the heavenly prize for which God, through Christ Jesus, is calling us."[2]

You can still be focused, fierce, and on fire as you strive toward not being broke and be content. I want to encourage you because this process is hard. You may be comparing your life to other people's lives and wonder why they have nicer houses, cars, clothes, jewelry, and vacations than you. Then, you may start to feel envy and jealousy toward other people because you are playing the comparison game. Take heed! Envy and jealousy are dangerous emotions that will lead you back to a life of living paycheck to paycheck just to keep up with other people's lifestyles. Don't let envy and jealousy sabotage your progress!

Two Enemies of Contentment: Envy and Jealousy

Envy and jealousy can cause you to stray from the path to maximize your money to not be broke. Here is how those two feelings could rear their ugly heads in your life. You may be strolling through your social media of choice (Facebook, Twitter, Instagram, and any other online social platform). You see one of your friend's Facebook pictures of her new house that she purchased on the "rich" side of town. She boasts that she bought it with no money down, fully furnished, and has a low monthly payment. Her pictures show the house, inside and outside, from various angles showcasing the house's elegance. Then, you think to yourself, "Why can't we buy a new house on the "good" side of town? Why are we still renting an apartment? What has she done to afford that house? I want to buy a house, too! Now, not later! Forget waiting!" You want to celebrate with your friend and let her know that you are excited for her. But, deep down inside you feel jealousy, anger, and resentment. A feeling of dislike starts to surface.

Then, your feelings go beyond jealousy to envy, which is when someone desires what another person has. In your mind and heart, you want your friend's house. Instead of trying to take her home (because that would be called theft), you forego the path to not be broke. Ultimately, straying away could lead you back to the land of living paycheck to paycheck. I urge you to be vigilant in keeping jealousy and envy at bay by being content. Getting caught up in comparing your life to other people's lives will cause you to make unwise money decisions.

The Remedy to Envy and Jealousy

How do you fight against becoming a victim of the "comparison game" and being swept away by the tide of envy and jealousy? The answer is with contentment. Scripture says, "Yet true godliness with contentment is itself great wealth."[3] One of the goals of maximizing your money is to lead you to become financially wealthy. Before reaching financial wealth, you must become content, which is great wealth according to Scripture. Contentment is the remedy to the emotions of jealousy and envy that you may experience.

An attitude of gratitude can help with becoming content as well. Being thankful for the blessings that you have is a great way to contentment. If you live in the United States of America, you are considered "rich." According to research, the average U.S. taxpayer's annual income is $38,923.[4] Many Americans may not agree with this statistic because they do not have a millionaire status; however, compared to the rest of the world, Americans are rich.

If you do not think that you are rich, let's make a list of several luxuries that people may have and see if you have them, too.

- Clean drinking water
- Air condition in your home
- Multiple automobiles
- Two pairs of shoes
- $38,923 or more annual income

You can continue this list and post it on your bathroom mirror as a reminder that you are rich and blessed more than most of the world's population. Gratitude is also a remedy to jealousy and envy because it allows you to realize that your needs are met and that you have more than enough material possessions; therefore, you do not need more things to make you happy. You will not be jealous or envious of your neighbor's new BMW or Mercedes Benz or your friend's new house because you are grateful for what has been entrusted to you.

As you continue on this financial journey, you may start to feel envious or jealous of other people. Or, you may compare your life to your friend's highlight reel on social media. When that happens, I encourage you to be grateful. Gratitude leads to contentment. Contentment leads to great wealth.

Ground Rules for Wealth Accumulation

Money has a special power that can cause people to act weird, even at a young age. When I was in middle school, I lived in a neighborhood that was by no means considered "wealthy." However, some of the children that I went to school with had a perception that they were better than other people because their parents earned a certain amount of money. One day, I heard one girl say that her mother does not shop at a certain big box retailer, implying that they were above shopping there. The girl perceived her family as being rich (which of course they probably were based on the discussion above). In actuality, her family was broke because they lived in the same neighborhood as me.

Now, imagine if the girl's family really was wealthy. How would she treat other people? Her ego would be huge! She would probably belittle others, be arrogant, and be very self-centered. Having money increases who you already are as a person. If you are prideful, conceited, and egotistical, then money would enhance those character flaws. On the other hand, if you are humble, caring, and selfless, then having money would increase those wonderful character attributes as well. As you accumulate wealth, I suggest checking in regularly with your loved ones or accountability partner to make sure the money is not changing you in a negative way. Managing wealth is a major responsibility. You want to have the character traits such as humility, honesty, compassion, love, and selflessness as your wealth builds because it can ruin you and your relationships.

You may have heard stories of people that receive an inheritance or wealth from their parents or even lottery winnings, and because those people did not have the character to handle the weight of the wealth, it ruined them. The wealth was not a blessing. It was a curse. So here are some ground rules to follow as you accumulate wealth.

1) Do not be a jerk (if you are a jerk before you accumulate wealth, you will be a bigger jerk with money).

2) Develop good character traits (see above).

3) Give (more to follow later in the book about giving).

What is Wealth?

One thing that I love to do is read books. The problem that I have with reading is that I read slow, which hinders me from reading a lot of books. However, by reading slow, I really get an opportunity to digest the book. One book that I read, *The Millionaire Next Door*, by Thomas Stanley, talks about wealth in the U.S. Stanley defines wealth as a net worth (i.e., value of one's assets less liabilities) of $1 million or more.[5] That is the number one followed by six zeros! That's a lot of money. What could you do for yourself, your family, and your community if you had $1 million? The possibilities are many! Having this level of wealth could allow you to start your own business, help a single mother pay her utility bills, send your grandchild to college, and more. You can become wealthy by following the steps outlined in this book. In fact, 80% of America's millionaires are first-generation rich.[6] That means you (yes, YOU!) can be wealthy as well! Here's how to accumulate wealth.

Work + Time + Discipline = Wealth

Work

To accumulate wealth, you must work. Without consistently working, no money can be earned to allow you to put into your investment account to grow wealth. The Bible says, "Lazy people want much but get little, but those who work will prosper."[7] You reap what you sow. If you do not work, you do not get paid; it's that simple. Whether you are self-employed or an employee, you can do this.

Both my parents worked when I was growing up, and I believe seeing them work motivated me to have a great work ethic. I started working when I was about fourteen years old and have worked since, so I know the value of work. Another element of wealth accumulation is your income level. The more money you earn, the faster you can build wealth. I encourage you, if possible, to start a small business doing something you love to earn income. Having a small business is a great way to have control of your financial destiny.

Time
I do not like to wait for my goals to come to fruition. I would rather skip the process and get the result. Life does not work that way though. Shameka has told me on many, many occasions that things take "time" to happen; as much as I did not like her statement, she was right. Chasing a dream takes time. Striving for a goal takes time. Building a house, a business, finishing school, you name it, takes TIME. Accumulating wealth is no different. Anything worth doing takes time. There is a process that must happen to accomplish a goal or objective. Wealth is grown over time, not overnight.

I worked with a lady that spent money trying to win the lottery; to protect her identity I will call her Lucy. Lucy told me that she had been playing the lottery since 1988. She has been playing the lottery for almost thirty years. That is a very long-time putting money in a vehicle that has a very low percent chance of you winning. Just think how much wealth she could have amassed during the time she has been playing the lottery? It is better to invest your money over time than to spend it on get-rich-quick schemes like the lottery or buying single stocks. An old Proverb states, "Wealth from get-rich-quick schemes quickly disappears; wealth from hard work grows over time."[8]

If you invest 10% to 15% of your income, like we teach, over time you will become wealthy. Wealth is accumulated slowly and steadily over time. It is a process; it is not a microwave process (i.e., cook food quickly). It is a crock-pot process (i.e., cook food slowly).

Discipline
One key element to achieving any goal is discipline. Whether you want to lose weight, build a business, earn a college degree, or any other worthwhile goal, discipline is part of the equation. Let's revisit the definition of discipline. Discipline is an activity, exercise, or a regimen that develops or improves a skill.[9] Discipline also involves doing a task in a systematic manner, consistently over time. Accumulating wealth takes discipline as well. If you combine discipline with determination, you can achieve any goal you set your mind to do. One example of discipline in my life is writing this book. I am disciplined in putting in the work to put the words in my mind on paper and am determined to get my message of hope out to the world. However, I am NOT disciplined in getting sleep! I need to work on that area of my life!

Scripture talks about discipline as well, which says, "To learn, you must love discipline; it is stupid to hate correction."[10] In other words, discipline helps us to learn and grow. It helps us to improve and correct any unproductive, negative behavior. The discipline in accumulating wealth is consistently investing in your stock mutual funds month after month, year after year for 10, 20, 30, or 40 years. Accumulating wealth is a marathon, not a sprint. You must have endurance during this process. Compare wealth building to preparing for a race. When you run a marathon, you must have the discipline to train on a regular basis to develop your stamina and endurance for the physical and emotional challenges that you will face as you run. Eating healthy food, drinking plenty of water, and staying positive and motivated are all disciplined tasks you need to perform during your training. In terms of wealth building, you must be disciplined in budgeting each month, hating and staying out of debt, keeping a mega Rainy Day Fund of three to nine months of living expenses, and funding your stock mutual funds consistently over time.

If you continue to work hard and are disciplined in handling money God's ways like we have discussed thus far and invest over time, you will accumulate wealth. Zig Ziglar said, "You plus God equals enough." He is right. You can do this!

Wealth

Earlier in the chapter I defined the meaning of wealth; that is, someone that has a net worth of $1 million or more. That's $1,000,000. That wealth could consist of cash, your primary residence, rental property, your business, and investments. According to Thomas Stanley, there were about 3.5 million households in America that are considered wealthy.[11] When you accumulate $1 million, you have opportunities and obligations. You have opportunities to bless other people that are less fortunate than you. Managing wealth is a major responsibility that should not be taken lightly. By having character to handle the wealth, you will be able to make a significant impact on others.

Addressing Self-Doubt and Haters

First, I want to congratulate you for making it this far on the journey to not be broke! You have come a long way to change your life. Take a bow! I want to give you permission to relax a LOT! You have worked hard to become savvy with money. With that being said, I need to address the issue of self-doubt regarding money. Some people think that if you have a lot of money that you are an evil person. Some may even quote Scripture saying, "For the love of money is the root of all kinds of evil."[12] Money is not bad, but loving money causes people to misbehave and act unethically and immorally. Money simply does not have any morals; therefore, it is not good or bad. People do good and bad things with money. One example that I recently read about involved a large bank. The bank managers set unrealistic sales goals for the employees to obtain, so employees were opening bank accounts without the customers' consent. Thus, the bank employees and managers behaved inappropriately for money. For the record: You are not a bad or evil person just because you managed money well enough to accumulate wealth.

Second, I will ensure you that people will not like that you have wealth. People are going to hate, so be prepared for jealousy from others. Some of those people may be your family members; they may despise you because of your wealth. More than likely the haters do not live within their means and are drowning in debt. When they see that you are living opposite of the culture, it is natural for jealousy and envy to take hold of their hearts and emotions. How do you combat haters? With love. In the end, you are described as being wise and your haters are the definition of a fool according to Scripture. "The wise have wealth and luxury, but fools spend whatever they get."[13]

You're Wealthy, Now What?

Now that you have amassed wealth, what's next? You are part of a small percent of the U.S. population that has managed God's resources in an honorable way. Wealth is a great responsibility, but it is also a great opportunity to let people see God's provision through you. Scripture talks about wealth and how to manage it. For example, Scripture says, "Good people leave an inheritance to their grandchildren."[14] You were wise in accumulating wealth, so let's discuss some ways to manage it.

Enjoy some of your money

Have you ever been on a cruise to the Bahamas or to a resort in Jamaica? I have been blessed to do both. My father-in-law and mother-in-law took Shameka and me on a cruise to the Bahamas before we got married. We enjoyed being on the water. While on the cruise ship, we experienced fine dining, excellent dinner options, entertainment, and a different culture.

In 2007, Shameka and I traveled to Ocho Rios, Jamaica and stayed in a hotel resort. We drove to Atlanta, Georgia to go to the airport and departed from there to Jamaica. After landing in Jamaica, we received our luggage at the local airport, and we traveled in a bus for about an hour on an unpaved road to the resort. An experience like that makes me grateful for paved roads. Specifically, I really liked playing volley ball in the swimming pool with the other guests and getting a chance to travel internationally.

Now, it's your turn! I encourage you to travel domestically and abroad to destinations that you have never been before. Invite family and friends to join you to create memorable moments that you will truly treasure for life. Or, maybe you want to spend time with your children and grandchildren since your daily schedule does not permit much family time. Enjoy the fruit of your labor with those you love; you have earned it!

Continue to budget

For a nerd guy like me, I enjoy budgeting! I have been budgeting consistently for about ten years, and I like keeping a pulse on our money. Honestly, I do not know how people do not budget their money. Budgeting has become a habit for Shameka and me. As you go through this financial journey, budgeting will become second nature to you as well. Once you hit the "millionaire status" I recommend that you continue to do a monthly budget. Why? Because in order to keep your wealth, you must continue to budget. Besides, why stop doing the very activity that helped you accumulate wealth? No matter how much wealth you build, you will never outgrow the need to budget your money.

Live a dream

One of my favorite poems, *Dreams*, was written by Langston Hughes. Despite the poem only being eight lines long, those lines are profound. Hughes talks about holding fast to one's dreams. He draws attention to the consequences of not holding on to dreams. The poet compares life to a broken winged bird and a barren field. If one does not hold fast to dreams, he will not be able to soar as a bird because of the broken wing. Or, his field will not produce the fruit that is meant to sprout from the ground because of the snow covered, barren field.

In essence, Hughes is urging people to never stop reaching for their dreams! No matter how difficult the path to achieving the dream is, do not give up. What dream do you need to rescue? Maybe you have a dream of starting a business, writing a book, adopting children, traveling to another country, learning a second language, becoming a surgeon, or starting a non-profit. Now that you have built wealth, you can clean the dust and cobwebs from your dream that has been placed on a bookshelf and create a plan of ACTION to make that dream become a reality. T.E. Lawrence said, "Dreamers of the Day are dangerous people because they act their dreams into reality with open eyes."

Plan to transfer wealth to heirs

This principle is one that should not be taken lightly. You have worked too hard and sacrificed too much to let someone else squander the wealth that you have accumulated. You want to leave an inheritance for your children and grandchildren, but if your descendants do not know how to manage money and have the character to carry the weight of the wealth, the wealth will ruin them and the inheritance will disappear in one generation. First, I suggest getting a will. A will is a document that allows you to tell others how you want your assets handled when you pass away. If you do not have a will when you pass away, the state court system will determine who gets your assets; you do not want the state taking care of your personal affairs. Be sure that your will is specific to the state that you live in. Therefore, if you do not want to leave your son an inheritance because he has a drug problem, then you can state those wishes in your will.

In addition to the will, I recommend getting a living will. A living will lets you tell your loved ones and other people how you want to be treated in the event you are hospitalized and cannot speak for yourself. For example, a living will gives you the chance to express whether or not you want to be connected to a respirator (a medical device that keeps you alive) even though your bodily functions have stopped working. This is a very important document that should be completed and discussed with your family.

Another document I suggest adding to your financial planning tool box is a Power of Attorney (POA). A POA enables you to select someone to represent you in personal matters in the event you are not able to talk or communicate. The executor, or the person you select, will be responsible for handling your personal affairs regarding your finances, banking information, and other matters. Be sure you choose someone you trust to be your POA.

Here's another suggestion. Before giving your children and grandchildren your hard-earned wealth, I suggest having them read this book and apply the principles to their lives. Once they have proven that they can manage their personal finances, I would include them in the will. Another incentive for your descendants to receive their inheritance is to require them to read this book each year. You want to help your children and grandchildren develop strong character traits, be able to manage the wealth responsibly, and allow it to grow and be passed to other generations.

In addition, you can transfer your assets to minors using the Uniform Gift to Minors Act (UGMA) or the Uniform Transfers to Minors Act (UTMA). According to Franklin Templeton, an investment company, most states have created these acts to allow adults to transfer assets to a minor.[15] The UGMA and the UTMA both are managed by a custodian, or someone that oversees the account on behalf of the minor, until the minor becomes 18 or 21 years of age. When the minor becomes the appropriate age, she will receive the assets and use them as she wants.

If the donor, whom may be the acting custodian as well, of the UGMA and/or the UTMA passes away before the assets are transferred to the minor, the assets may be taxable as part of the donor's estate. There is one major difference between the UGMA and UTMA regarding what assets are allowed to be transferred to the minor. The UTMA allows all types of assets including real estate, to be transferred to a minor; the UGMA only permits gifts or transfers of cash and securities.[16]

Another option is to transfer assets to your desired beneficiaries by establishing a trust. A trust is a document that states how you, the grantor, want your assets to be managed and distributed to your beneficiaries. You can set up a trust while you are living or upon your death via a will. A living trust can be revocable (changeable) or irrevocable (unchangeable).[17] Anyone with assets can set up a trust; however, creating a trust is a lengthy process. Consult a professional estate attorney or financial planner to set up a trust.

In addition, a trustee (that you select) manages the trust on behalf of the beneficiary. At your death, the trustee will pay all of your final obligations such as expenses, taxes, and debts and transfer the remaining assets to your beneficiaries.[18] I recommend using the UGMA, UTMA (preferably), or a trust to transfer your wealth to your children and grandchildren.

Protect your wealth with an umbrella insurance policy
Have you ever heard the term "Gold Digger?" Well, when I was growing up, guys would call a girl that only wanted money and material possessions a gold digger. I assume the term was derived from the gold rush of 1849, where people fled to find gold in California. A gold digger girl only wanted to be with a guy because he had money, nice clothes, and a sporty car. (By the way, men can be considered as gold diggers, too). When you become wealthy, people may become gold diggers seeking to get your money.

One way people may try to take your wealth is through "intentional" accidents. Let me explain. Imagine if your neighbor, Allison, knows you have accumulated wealth and becomes jealous of your financial success. Instead of asking you what steps you took to build wealth, she creates a plan to have an intentional accident. One day she is leaving for work and knows that you leave for work at about the same time. As she drives to work, she gets in front of you before going through a stop light. Just before the light changes to yellow to signal traffic to slow down before the light changes to red to stop traffic, you press the accelerator to get through the light. However, the person in the car in front of you (i.e., your neighbor) slams on the brakes causing you to collide into the rear of the car! Her perfect plan is executed! You get out of the car to go check on the person you rear-ended. As you approach the car you hear, "Whip lash! Whip lash!" You look in the car and realize that it is Allison. Not ready for a lawsuit? Well, get ready for a lawsuit from her in an attempt to take your wealth.

Here's another example. You own a rental property, and you have an insurance policy of $500,000 to cover any injuries on the property. There is one problem tenant, Zachary, that pays his rent on time each month, but he complains about various matters concerning the property maintenance. Zachary has heard that you have built wealth over the years and wants a piece of your pie. One day, you receive a phone call that he stepped into a pothole on your property and broke his ankle. Despite your efforts to have the pothole repaired, it did not get fixed. You discussed the matter with your maintenance crew and were told that repairing the pothole was not a priority when the repair was initiated. Zachary threatens to sue you for neglecting to fix the pothole. He plans to get a lawyer to sue you for $1,000,000, which is more than your insurance coverage. Again, are you ready to fight against a lawsuit? How will you be able to pay the additional $500,000 if the tenant wins the case?

      Those are just some situations that could happen to you because of jealous people; remember we talked about envy and jealousy earlier? In order to protect yourself and your wealth against gold diggers, I recommend getting an umbrella insurance policy. An umbrella insurance policy is additional insurance above your normal insurance policy. For example, in the story above you already had $500,000 of insurance coverage, and if you had a $1,000,000 umbrella insurance policy the umbrella policy would pay the additional $500,000 above the normal policy (i.e., $1,000,000 - $500,000 = $500,000). I highly recommend getting an umbrella insurance policy of at least $1,000,000 to protect your wealth from being taken by gold diggers.

Establish a team of professional advisors

I mentioned getting professionals to assist you with insurance, investments, real estate, and other areas. I recommended finding professionals that care about you, have your best interest in mind, and are willing to educate you on the subject matter. As you accumulate wealth, you will have questions regarding estate planning, wealth transfer, insurance, and other topics. With a team of professional advisors, their expert advice will help you make more informed decisions concerning your wealth.

      The professionals are there to give you guidance and be a sounding board for you. Ultimately, you need to make the decisions regarding your money. The knowledge that you have gained through this book coupled with your team of professionals is to empower you to make wise financial decisions. I recommend not delegating the responsibility of managing your wealth to someone else, unless you are not physically and mentality capable of doing it yourself.

Your important documents

We have talked a lot about wealth and about ways to manage it. Eventually, a time is going to come when you will have to leave it to someone else to manage. When that time comes, you want to ensure that your loved ones can find the important documents regarding your money and other areas of your life. I recommend creating a file to store your important documents such as your will, living will, POA, insurance policies, bank account information, rental property information, and any other vital documents that your family members will need in the event of your death.

Shameka and I have a tote bag with our important documents should each of us need it. This is one way that we show our love for each other. If I die, Shameka will know where to find my life insurance policy and other important documents. A suggestion is to keep your file locked in a fireproof safe.

Help other people by giving

The final way I suggest to spend your wealth is by giving. Giving is a great way to express how much you care for other people. Let's discuss giving in more detail in the next chapter.

Action Steps to Maximize Your Money to Stop Being Broke

1. Have fun spending some of your wealth with your family and friends.
2. Talk to a professional insurance agent about protecting your wealth with an umbrella insurance policy. As always, understand the policy before making a purchase.
3. Make plans to transfer your wealth to your heirs. Consider establishing a trust, UTMA, or UGMA.
4. Create your file of important documents today! Discuss it with your spouse or accountability partner.

Living Generously
Looking Beyond Yourself

Have you ever had someone bless you unexpectedly? I am sure almost everyone has received a surprise gift from a loved one or a total stranger. My pastor, Craig Groeschel, talks about how he received a gift from his grandmother that he did not expect. One of my memorable moments of receiving an unexpected gift was during my final year of undergraduate study in college in Kentucky. In fact, I received this gift shortly after graduating.

Being a broke college kid just finishing a very challenging and difficult four years itself was my gift to myself! Shortly after graduation, I was walking across campus taking care of final tasks to close out my tenure at the college. A gentleman I had never met approached me and asked me my name; I told him. As we talked, he said that the college's Business Department selected one student from the students in the department that professors felt was an exemplary student. Out of more than several hundred students, the department chose me. Then, he presented me with a check for about nine hundred dollars! That totally caught me off guard, definitely unexpected! I used the money to help with moving expenses to move back home after college. Money put to good use I must say. Not only have I received unexpected gifts of money, but gifts of kindness and support as well. In life, I am convinced that everyone needs someone to provide support along life's journey. One special person in my life that showed me an unexpected gift of assistance, support, and love is Montina Wesley, my former psychology professor. By her intersecting my life, I am a better man, and my life is more enriched. Had Montina not given of herself to help me unlock the potential stored within me, I would not be where I am today, I would not be married to my beautiful wife, Shameka, and I would not have a cute daughter.

Giving: Why Is It Important?
As we discuss the topic of giving, I want you to understand its importance as you move toward not being broke. Being a follower of Jesus Christ, I want to look at giving from a Christian worldview. Even if you are not a follower of Christ, I ensure you that these principles can apply to you as well. First, we must understand our position in the big scheme of life. According to Scripture, God owns everything. "The earth is the Lord's, and everything in it. The world and all its people belong to him."[1] Wow!

That means everything from our health to our wealth belongs to God! Therefore, God is the owner, and we are managers of his assets. We are just managing God's belongings for him. He has entrusted us with this responsibility; that is why it is so important that we manage the wealth that we have earned because it's God's property. Think of yourself as a manager of God's assets to do good things for other people for God. So here is a principle that I want you to understand and keep in your mind and in your heart: God is the OWNER. We are the MANAGERS.

If we remember this principle, as we accumulate wealth and we increase our lifestyles, the things we own will not own us because we know our position. God thinks highly of us enough to entrust us with his stuff! In fact, Scripture proves my point. "What are mere mortals that you should think about them, human beings that you should care for them? Yet you made them only a little lower than God and crowned them with glory and honor. You gave them charge of everything you made, putting all things under their authority."[2]

Tithing: The Minimum Giving Principle

As followers of Jesus, Christians are called to give a tenth of their income, also known as the tithe. My pastor, Craig Groeschel, says "Giving is not what we do, it's who we are." The tithe is mentioned throughout Scripture. For example, the Bible states, "One tenth of the produce of the land whether grain from the fields or fruit from the trees, belongs to the Lord and must be set apart to him as holy."[3] Years ago, many of the people were farmers, so Scripture used words that they could understand. In addition, the Bible gives instructions regarding the tithe. "Bring all the tithes into the storehouse so there will be enough food in my Temple. If you do, says the Lord, I will open the windows of heaven for you. I will pour out a great blessing so great you won't have enough room to take it in! Try it! Put me to the test!"[4] Let's discuss this in further detail.

If we understand that God owns everything, then giving something that does not belong to us should not be that hard. What happens when we tithe? First, it allows us to put God first in our lives and highlights who really owns our resources. Second, the tithe meets the needs of the local church. The Temple represents the church and where God dwelt in the Old Testament. Today, the local church is a symbol of the Temple. When the local church receives tithes from Christ followers, or its members, the needs of the church are met. Lastly, when people tithe, God blesses them! Blessings can come in different forms: Financial, relational, spiritual, emotional, and physical. If you do not believe, then "Try it," Scripture says!

In addition, giving a tithe is an act of worship. Scripture describes it like this: "You must set aside a tithe of your crops – one-tenth of all the crops you harvest each year. Bring this tithe to the designated place of worship – the place the Lord your God chooses for his name to be honored."[5] When we tithe, we are worshipping God with our finances, and that says a lot about our character. Why? Because giving is not something we naturally do, even as Christians. In his book, *The Treasure Principle*, Randy Alcorn discusses giving from a biblical perspective, and he states, "Nearly every study indicates that American Christians give on average between 2% and 3% of their income."[6] In other words, many Christians don't tithe. We give only a small percentage of our income back to the church. My hope is that as you apply the steps of not being broke, your giving will increase over time. Maybe that 2% to 3% will increase to 10% or more! In fact, as you look at the Monthly Money Plan, the first line item is giving! So over time, giving will become a habit for you.

Scripture also talks about an "offering" in addition to the tithe. "You have cheated me of the tithes and offerings due to me."[7] An offering is giving of your income in addition to the tithe. The offering comes from surplus; therefore, any additional money that you give beyond tithing would be considered an offering. If you have given a tithe to your local church, and you feel led to give an offering to help a single mother that is struggling to feed her two children, by all means do it!

Why Give?

Great question! I am glad you asked. Let me illustrate a point. Say you have a son, Langston, who is great at helping other people become better at using their talents and gifts. He does a fabulous job in school academically and excels at extracurricular activities such as basketball, soccer, and swimming. Langston volunteers with the Boys and Girls Club in your community and works a part-time job.

Then, there is your neighbor's son, Nicholas, who is the total opposite of Langston. Nicholas has the wrong friends that pressure him to do things like steal, vandalize, and commit robbery. One day, Nicholas and his friends are at a liquor store buying alcohol with a fake identification (I.D.) card. When they try to buy alcohol, the store clerk asks for an I.D.; one of Nicholas's friends displays the I.D. However, the clerk notices something suspicious about the I.D. and does not allow the boys to buy the liquor. One of the boys pulls out a gun and points it at the clerk and demands that the clerk let them make a purchase. Scared out of his wits, the clerk agrees to let the boys buy the liquor. Instead of paying for the liquor, Nicholas and his friends run out of the store without paying for it. Immediately the clerk calls the police to report the incident.

Eventually, Nicholas and his friends are arrested and are sentenced to go to jail for five years. However, you hear what happened to Nicholas and the gang and are moved with compassion for them. You and

Langston have a heart-to-heart conversation about this situation, and Langston agrees to go to jail for Nicholas's crime instead of Nicholas going to jail. He knows that if Nicholas goes to jail, his parents will be devastated. Langston decides to take punishment for a crime that he did not commit.

Alright, I know that this story is farfetched. You may be thinking, "What parent in her right mind would let her child pay the price for someone else's crime?" I agree with you and probably do not know anyone that would give her one and only child for a person that deserved punishment. However, I know someone that did: God. The Bible tells us that "For this is how God loved the world: He gave his one and only Son, so that everyone who believes in him will not perish but have eternal life."[8] God did what you and I could never imagine doing; he made a huge sacrifice. Why? Because he loved the world. That means God loves YOU! Jesus Christ's sacrifice for a world that did not deserve his love is the reason for giving. God gave first, so as a follower of Christ, my only reasonable response is to give. The tithe represents our response to God's gift of salvation.

Tithing also has a benefit for the giver. When we tithe, we become more like Jesus. God wants us to become more like him and Jesus Christ. Tithing helps develop our character making us less self-centered and molds us to become others-centered. Becoming selfless takes work and effort because naturally we are selfish people. You do not have to teach a child to be selfish; by his very nature, he is selfish. Tithing breaks the self-centeredness and frees us to be generous to let blessings flow through us to meet the needs of other people. By tithing, you are being obedient to return to God what he already owns, and your heart, mind, and soul are transformed to make you become who you were designed to be.

Before I really understood the tithe, I despised tithing because I thought that the church that I attended was using the money to fund its "building fund." I did not want to give to a church that was going to use "my money" to contribute to a larger facility. Well, God does not really need my money to fulfill his will. He can just take it! It's his! I voiced my feelings to one of my aunts, Sylvia, about tithing, and she directed me to Scripture that discussed the building of the Tabernacle, which represented God's house. She told me that there is nothing wrong with using tithes to build a "big" church. When I searched Scripture, specifically Exodus, I saw that God had instructed the Israelites, his chosen people, to build him an elaborate home. The Israelites were commanded to use gold, silver, bronze, and fine goatskin leather, in building the Tabernacle. My aunt was right. God did not want some rinky-dink shack to live in; he wanted the best of course! He's God! If my tithe goes toward building a larger building to reach more lost and hurting people, then I am on board with giving my share to make it happen.

If you are not convinced to start tithing or giving, then I hope I can convince you with these words. Picture your life ten years from today. You have $10,000 saved in your Rainy Day Fund, no debt (AWESOME!), have $500,000 in your IRA, and have a paid for house (i.e., no mortgage, baby!). Who could you bless? Where would you travel to for vacation? How much would you give to charity or donate to a cause of your choice? How much would you spend on a "new" used car? The possibilities are many! I am convinced that if you apply the principles that we have discussed in this book to your life, the picture we just painted could be your reality.

When your basic needs are met, you have the ability to focus on meeting the needs of the people in your community and even extend your reach to help other people around the world. But when you are living paycheck to paycheck and are worried about how you will pay your bills, you are not free to bless others financially. Jesus said, "It is more blessed to give than to receive."[9] Not only will the person you are helping receive a blessing, you will be blessed as well! Giving is a win-win situation! All parties benefit from the experience.

This whole giving process is purging us of selfishness. As you work hard to accumulate wealth, I want you to enjoy the fruit of your labor. I also encourage you to make giving a lifestyle. Author, speaker, and human trafficking advocate, Christine Caine, talks about giving of your time, treasure, talent, and tongue in a sermon she did at my church. Be generous with your time by investing in your family and friends to create lasting relationships and memories. Volunteer in your community at a local non-profit that shares some of your personal values. Everyone is gifted with a natural talent that can be used to meet the needs of other people. I encourage you to use that gift to enrich someone else's life. Whether you have a gift of writing, speaking, drawing, singing, or solving problems, use it to uplift people in your life. If you do not know your talent, seek it out; pray, look within yourself, read books, and get Godly counsel for guidance. Words are powerful. They have the power to uplift or destroy, to enflame or extinguish. Use your words to inject positivity into your life and hope into others. Last but not least, make tithing a priority and giving a habit as you move toward not being broke.

As we close this chapter on giving, let me share my tithing story with you. When I attended a Baptist church back home in South Carolina, I began to tithe. I felt good that I was able to tithe. However, as time passed, I was not tithing consistently. After getting married and relocating to Oklahoma, something changed for the better. Shameka got a job offer in Oklahoma, and I left two jobs in South Carolina and arrived in

Oklahoma jobless. We decided not to stay separated from each other for a year (with her living in Oklahoma and me living in South Carolina) because of the possibility of marital problems that we did not want to encounter living away from each other. Well, as we started attending the new church in Oklahoma, the topic of tithing was addressed. Shameka and I discussed it. She wanted to tithe (even with me not working), but I was hesitant. Shameka had faith, while I had fear. We talked with a pastor at the church about finding work for me, and Shameka and I decided to tithe. That was the fall of 2012; since then, we have been consistently tithing to our local church. God is faithful. He has blessed us in more ways than we ever could have imagined financially. Specifically, Shameka and I prayed to have children; my wife prayed to God to give her her heart's desire. He honored her prayer and gave us Naomi.

You see, one reason that I teach people about budgeting, destroying debt, saving for unexpected events, paying off their homes, and accumulating wealth is to empower them to GIVE! Nothing that I have belongs to me! My wife, daughter, clothes, shoes, cars, and my life belong to God. I want to give my time, talent, tongue, and treasure to serve other people and to bring God glory. I hope you are convinced to do the same.

Action Steps to Maximize Your Money to Stop Being Broke
1. Do a self-analysis and identify any selfishness in your life.
2. If you are not already tithing, decide to start tithing for ninety days.
3. Consider giving an offering in addition to your tithe.

12
Never Going to be Broke Again!
Hope and a Bright Future

In the introduction of this book, I discussed the meaning of hope. Let's revisit it here. Hope is the feeling that what is wanted can be had or that events will turn out for the best.[1] People need hope in all seasons of life. One thing that I have learned is that life is hard, and when people lose hope they give up on life. Whether you started reading this book already hope-filled or began hopeless, there is hope for you today. I wrote this book for people to learn to handle money God's ways, so that they could become who they were created to become to bless other people. H.O.P.E. ultimately means helping other people become empowered through financial literacy. That is the mission of my company because people need hope. People are struggling, living paycheck to paycheck, and marriages are being destroyed because of the lack of financial literacy, which leads to people losing hope.

Yes, this book is about personal finances. But it is so much more. This whole process of budgeting, crushing debt, saving for unexpected events, retirement, and accumulating wealth is important not only for your financial well-being. These principles are vital to your relationships with your spouse, children, friends, family, community, and the world at large. These are the reasons we must get this stuff right!

Never Going to be Broke Again: The Final Destination
Helen Keller said, "Optimism is the faith that leads to achievement. Nothing can be done without hope and confidence." She is right. Nothing can be done if you do not have hope that it can be done. Your personal finances cannot be better without hope. Your marriage will not improve without hope. Your children, health, career, business, or community cannot and will not prosper without hope. In spite of life's difficulties, you have to believe that your circumstances can and will change. In the book, *Good to Great*, author Jim Collins talks about the Stockdale Paradox, which states, "Retain faith that you will prevail in the end, regardless of the difficulties, AND, at the same time confront the most brutal facts of your current reality, whatever they might be."[2] In other words, Collins is saying have hope while acknowledging your current situation. If you have hope, you can turn a bad situation into a superb situation.

When you follow the principles outlined in this book, you will not be financially broke. Not living paycheck to paycheck and having your financial house in order opens opportunities for you to focus on the important things in life. You can focus on becoming who God created you to become! The Bible says, "For we are God's masterpiece. He created us anew in Christ Jesus, so we can do the good things he planned for us long ago."[3] God has a plan and purpose for your life. It's not by accident. This is one of the reasons I want to share this message of hope because people need to know that they are important and that they have a purpose. That purpose is in becoming who they were designed to become and being a tool to help enrich other people's lives. That's the essence of Broke: Helping Other People become Empowered to ultimately be a blessing!

The Next Level

I hope you have realized that this journey is not all about you and me. It's about meeting the needs of the world. Now that you understand what Broke is all about, here are some practical steps to go to the next level by applying what you learned.

1. Use your treasure, time, talent, and tongue to bless other people. Scripture says, "Use your freedom [in Christ] to serve one another in love."[4]
2. Live out your purpose by following the steps in Broke. You can do this!
3. Reread this book often. Share it with your family, friends, co-workers, and community.
4. Live focused, fierce, and on fire! Be intentional about your finances, relationships, spiritual well-being, health, business/career, emotions, and personal development.

My job is done. I have poured myself into this book, and I hope you will use the principles to change your life. I saw a quote on a vehicle that said, "One Life. Live It." You have one life, so live it wisely.

"Limits like fears are often just an illusion." – Michael Jordan

"Living on a monthly budget, giving, saving, investing, and spending wisely is the only way to live."

Epilogue

Thank you for allowing me to share this message of Broke with you. I would like to share another message of hope as our time together comes to an end.

I grew up going to church. My family and I attended my dad's church, which was a small Baptist church in Greenville, South Carolina. The choir consisted of men and women, and the pastor's wife played the piano; no other instruments were used in the choir as the pastor did not believe in the church having any other instruments (so I heard). On Sunday mornings, my mom and dad took us to church, and we sang hymnals along with the choir. The church service was a traditional Baptist format.

When my siblings and I visited my Aunt Sylvia, she always made us go to the church she attended. Her church consisted of a large choir, drums, guitars, and tambourines. Although the church was a Baptist church, the choir knew how to express themselves through worship. My aunt's church was very different than my dad's church in the worship style. Sometimes hymnals were sung, but often times songs were sang from memory. And, the church members were extremely expressive in their worship! Totally different from my dad's church!

As I grew older and went to college in Kentucky, I did not attend a regular church service. Although I had attended church and had been baptized, which is when you are immersed under water to symbolize your confession of faith, I was not truly dedicated to the Christian faith. Then, on September 11, 2011, that changed.

I knew about Jesus Christ, but did not totally become a fully-devoted follower of Jesus Christ (as my pastor Craig Groeschel says). I knew that God loved me, and the only way to get to God was through his Son, Jesus. I also knew that I had done hurtful things to other people and that I was a mess of a man. I needed Jesus Christ in my life. I asked him to forgive me for the bad things I had done and to be my Lord and Savior. That was the best decision that I ever made!

If you do not already know this, I want to tell you now. God loves you! I know this because he gave his only Son, Jesus Christ, to die for your sins and mine. None of us deserve God's love, grace, and mercy, but because he loves us, Jesus died and rose from the dead, so that we could be made right with God, our sins (or wrongful actions) could be forgiven, and we become part of God's family.

If you want to accept Jesus Christ as your Lord and Savior today, say this simple prayer with me:

"Heavenly Father, it's me. I know that I have fallen short of your standard. I have done wrong and have hurt other people. I confess that Jesus Christ is Lord, and I believe that you rose him from the dead. Please forgive me for my sins. Wash me in the blood of your Son, Jesus Christ. Make me whole and new. From this day forward, I will follow you. I love you Father. I love you Jesus. I pray in the name of Jesus. Amen."

If you said that prayer in sincerity, I want to welcome you to God's family! Your next steps are to get connected with a church in your community, and start to get to know him through studying Scripture and connecting with other believers of Jesus.

Jesus Christ is the true hope in your finances and in life. If you do not have a relationship with him, I encourage you to ask questions and get your questions answered to help you move in the direction of developing a relationship with him. He has a plan and purpose for your life.

About the Author

Dakota Grady is a money coach and speaker. He has led his personal finance class, *6 Steps to Maximize Your Money*, to help people to become better managers of their money and has coached many families and individuals how to get control of their finances and eliminate debt. He is on a crusade to bring HOPE by Helping Other People become Empowered through biblically-based financial literacy. Since 2010, Dakota has coached people how to create a budget, crush debt, save for unexpected events, and to move toward their financial goals.

Dakota knows what it feels like to struggle financially. He grew up in a low-income family of nine, living on welfare. There was a time that he and his siblings lived with their grandmother because they did not have electricity in their home. Dakota was determined not to live a life of financial hardship when he became an adult. When he became an adult, Dakota realized that he had a gift of handling money wisely.

Dakota is using his gift of smart money management to coach people to transform their lives. He is passionate about helping people handle money in ways that are biblical, and he can show you how you too can be smart with money. Dakota has a bachelor's degree in accounting and a bachelor's degree in marketing. In addition to being passionate about personal finance, Dakota loves reading, spending time with family, and swimming.

Connect with Dakota on Facebook, Instagram, LinkedIn, and online at dakotagrady.com.

Broke Money Management Forms
Monthly Money Plan

Help! It's a budget! Yes, this is the plan that you will use to tell your money how to behave. Each month is different, so each month requires a new budget.

First, enter your monthly earnings in the monthly earnings section. This would be the total amount of income you bring home (for you and your spouse if you are married).

Second, put the amount you plan to spend for each major category; some items have subcategories. For example, if you plan to spend $400 for the month on groceries and $80 for dining out, put those amounts in each category. Then, add both categories together and put the total amount in the planned total column.

Third, enter the total earnings in the Total Earnings section on page 3. Next, add up all of the categories, and put the total amount in the Total Planned Spending section. Then, subtract the Total Spending amount from the Total Earnings amount. The amount in the Remaining to Plan section should be zero.

Fourth, at the end of the month, insert the total amount spent in each category (or subcategory). This will let you know how to plan for preparing your budget for the next month. Some categories may need to be adjusted.

Monthly Money Plan

Month/Year

Monthly Earnings (After-Taxes)

Category	Planned	Spent	Left Over
GIVING (Suggested Percentage: 10%)			
Local Church (10%)			
Charitable Organization			
Planned Total			
PIGGY BANK (10% - 15%)			
Rainy Day Fund			
Golden Years (10% - 15%)			
School (2 Year or 4 Year College)			
Planned Total			
HOME (25% - 30%)			
Mortgage(s)			
Apartment/House Rent			
Property Taxes			
Home Owner's Association Fees			
Repairs			
Planned Total			
UTILITY BILLS			
Electricity			
Water			
Cell Phone			
Internet			
Cable			
Trash			
Planned Total	-		
FOOD/DINING (5% - 15%)			
Supermarket			
Out to Eat			
Planned Total			
CLOTHES			
Mom & Dad			
Kids			
Housekeeping/Washing & Drying			
Planned Total			
TRANSPORTATION (15 - 17%)			
Tags			
Gas			
Oil Change/Maintenance			
Tires			
Car Upgrade			
Planned Total			

INSURANCE

Automobile
Renter's/Homeowners
Health
Life
Dental
ID Theft Protection
LT Disability

Planned Total

WELL-BEING

Meds
Doctor Visits (Co-Pay)
Dental Visit (Co-Pay)
Vision
Supplements (Protein Shake)

Planned Total

HYGIENE/"UP KEEP"

Tissue/Soap/Toothpaste
Hair Products/Cut/"Do"
Make-up
Daycare/Baby Sitter
School Tuition
Personal Development
Membership Dues
Presents (Birthday, Holidays)
Home Furnishings
Her Splurge Money
His Splurge Money
Baby Needs
Animal Needs
Gadgets/Games/Music Downloads
Extra Curricular (Sports, Music, Dance, Other)

Planned Total

LEISURE

Travel
Fun!!

Planned Total

WHAT YOU OWE!!

Student Loan
Car Loan
Truck Loan
Credit Card Company 1
Credit Card Company 2
Medical Debt
Finance Company
Title/Pay Day Loan

Planned Total

LEFT OVER (To use for bills for beginning of next month)

119

Total Earnings

Minus: Total Planned Spending _____

Remaining to Plan ════════

Money Distribution Plan

Don't let this form scare you. The Money Distribution Plan, in simple terms, is just a way for you to know when to spend your money. This is where you "live" on the amounts from your Money Plan.

You will use the amounts from your Money Plan and break down the earnings and spending categories by pay period. It's a fun process, so let's get started!

First, put the pay date for each pay period in the Pay Date section. If you are paid every other week, put 1/1 and 1/15, for example.

Second, fill in the amount you are paid in the Pay Amount section.

Third, put the amount of money you have budgeted from your Money Plan in the Planned column, and subtract that amount from the Total Earnings for that pay period. There should be a running total of earnings remaining after the budgeted item, so that you know how much is left to spend for that pay period. That remaining amount should be in the Leftover column.

Fourth, continue going down the list until the "Leftover" column is equal to zero, which means all of your pay for that pay period has been spent on purpose.

Fifth, if there is money in the Leftover column, adjust your categories until the Leftover column is zero; every dollar of your pay should be put in a category. An alternative is to leave the remaining balance in the Leftover column and roll the balance forward to the following month. So the remaining balance will be included in the income amount on next month's budget.

Money Distribution Plan

Total Income _____

	Pay Date	MM/DD/YYYY		MM/DD/YYYY		MM/DD/YYYY		MM/DD/YYYY	
	Pay Amount								
CATEGORY		Planned	Left Over	Planned	Left Over	Planned	Left Over	Planned	Left Over
GIVING									
Local Church (10%)									
Charitable Organization									
PIGGY BANK									
Rainy Day Fund									
Retirement									
College (2 Year or 4 Year College)									
HOME									
Mortgage(s)									
Apartment/House Rent									
Property Taxes									
Home Owner's Association Fees									
Repairs									
UTILITY BILLS									
Electricity									
Water									
Cell Phone									
Internet									
Cable									
Trash									
FOOD/DINING									
Supermarket									
Out to Eat									
CLOTHES									
Mom & Dad									
Kids									
Housekeeping/Washing & Drying									
TRANSPORTATION									
Tags									
Gas									
Oil Change/Maintenance									
Tires									
Car Upgrade									

	Pay Date	Pay Date	Pay Date	Pay Date
INSURANCE				
Automobile				
Renter's/Homeowners				
Health				
Life				
Dental				
ID Theft Protection				
LT Disability				
WELL-BEING				
Meds				
Doctor Visits (Co-Pay)				
Dental Visit (Co-Pay)				
Vision				
Supplements (Protein Shake)				
HYGIENE/"UP KEEP"				
Tissue/Soap/Toothpaste/Other				
Hair Products/Cut/"Do"				
Make-up				
Daycare/Baby Sitter				
School Tuition				
Personal Development				
Membership Dues				
Presents (Birthday, Holidays)				
Home Furnishings				
Her Splurge Money				
His Splurge Money				
Baby Needs				
Animal Needs				
Gadgets/Games/Music Downloads				
Extra Curricular (Sports, Music, Dance, Other)				
LEISURE				
Travel				
Fun!!				
WHAT YOU OWE!!				
Student Loan				
Car Loan				
Truck Loan				
Credit Card Company 1				
Credit Card Company 2				
Medical Debt				
Finance Company				
Title/Pay Day Loan				
LEFT OVER				

Debt Crusher Method

The simplest way to eliminate debt is to use the Debt Crusher Method.

First, list your debts in order of tiniest to the biggest regardless of the interest rate. Pay the minimum required monthly payment on each debt. Pay as much as you can on the tiniest debt to crush it quickly.

Then, apply the amount you were paying on the first debt to the second debt to crush it. So the minimum payment you paid on debt #1 will be added to the minimum payment of debt #2 (and any extra money you can pay).

Continue this process for each debt. As you pay off each debt on your list, you will have more money to pay on the next debt. Continue crushing debt until you have completely destroyed your debt to become debt free!

Debt Crusher Method

Who You Owe	Total Owed	Required Minimum Payment	New Payment Amount for Pay Off	# of Payments for Pay Off

Notes

Introduction

1. "Hope". *Dictionary.com Unabridged.* Random House, Inc. 15 Jun. 2017. <Dictionary.com http://www.dictionary.com/browse/hope.

Chapter One

1. "Discipline." *Dictionary.com Unabridged.* Random House, Inc. 17 Jun. 2017. <Dictionary.com http://www.dictionary.com/browse/discipline?s=t.
2. Terry Felber. *The Legend of the Monk and the Merchant: Principles for Successful Living.* Nashville: World, 2004, 86.
3. Jeff Ostrowski. "Bankrate Survey: Fewer than 4 in 10 Americans could pay a surprise $1,000 bill from savings." Bankrate. 11 Jan. 2021. 10 Jul. 2021. https://www.bankrate.com/banking/savings/financial-security-january-2021/.
4. Dale Carnegie. *How to Win Friends and Influence People: The Only Book You Need to Lead You to Success.* New York: Gallery, 1936, xxi.

Chapter Two

1. Proverbs 24:27, NLT.
2. Elizabeth Bernstein. "Divorce's Guide to Marriage." *The Wall Street Journal.* 24 Jul. 2012. 20 Jul. 2021 https://www.wsj.com/articles/SB10000872396390444402520457754495 1717564114.
3. "Living Paycheck to Paycheck is a Way of Life for Majority of U.S. Workers, According to New Career Builder Survey." *Career Builder.* 24 Aug. 2017. 20 Jul. 2021. http://press.careerbuilder.com/2017-08-24-Living-Paycheck-to-Paycheck-is-a-Way-of-Life-for-Majority-of-U-S-Workers-According-to-New-CareerBuilder-Survey.
4. Dennis Jacobe. "One in Three Americans Prepare a Detailed Household Budget." *Gallup.* 3 Jun. 2013. 15 Jun. 2017. http://www.gallup.com/poll/162872/one-three-americans-prepare-detailed-household-budget.aspx.
5. Thomas J. Stanley, and William D. Danko. *The Millionaire Next Door: The Surprising Secrets of America's Wealthy.* Taylor Trade Publishing, 2010, p. 38.

Chapter Three

1. Cheryl R. Cooper. "The Debt Collection Market and Selected Policy Issues." *Congressional Research Service.* 22 Jun. 2021. 20 Jul. 2021. https://fas.org/sgp/crs/misc/R46477.pdf.
2. Proverbs 22:7, NLT.
3. "Depreciation Infographic: How Fast Does My New Car Lose Value?" *Edmunds.* May 2017. 20 Jul. 2021. https://forums.edmunds.com/discussion/26023/editorial/x/depreciation-infographic-how-fast-does-my-new-car-lose-value.
4. Melinda Zabritski. "Automotive Industry Insights: Finance Market Report Q2 2020." *Experian Information Solution, Inc.* 9 Nov. 2020. 22 Jul. 2021. https://www.experian.com/content/dam/marketing/na/automotive/quarterly-webinars/credit-trends/2020-q2-safm-final.pdf
5. "Consumer Information: Payday Loans." *Federal Trade Commission.* 2021 May. 22 Jul. 2021. https://www.consumer.ftc.gov/articles/0097-payday-loans.
6. Proverbs 22:7, NLT
7. Proverbs 22:26-27, NLT.
8. Ibid.

Chapter Four

1. Jeff Ostrowski. "Survey: Fewer than 4 in 10 Americans could pay a surprise $1,000 bill from savings." *Bankrate.* 11 Jan. 2021. 22 Jul. 2021. https://www.bankrate.com/banking/savings/financial-security-january-2021/.

Chapter Five

1. Goran Dautovic. "The 45 Most Important Advertising Statistics of 2021." *Small Biz Genius.* 27 Jan. 2021. 7 Aug. 2021. https://www.smallbizgenius.net/by-the-numbers/advertising-statistics/#gref.
2. Brad Adgate. "Measuring The Effectiveness of Radio Advertising in Connected Cars." *Forbes.* 9 Oct. 2020. 7 Aug. 2020. https://www.forbes.com/sites/bradadgate/2020/10/09/measuring-the-effectiveness-of-radio-advertising-in-connected-cars/?sh=7cece3de5fc7.
3. Utpal Dholakia. "Does It Matter Whether You Pay With Cash Or A Credit Card: Are there any downsides to using credit cards instead of cash?" *Psychology Today.* 11 Jul. 2016. 24 Aug. 2021. https://www.psychologytoday.com/blog/the-science-behind-behavior/201607/does-it-matter-whether-you-pay-cash-or-credit-card
4. Martin Lindstrom. "90 Percent Of All Purchasing Decisions Are Made Subconsciously." *ISPO News.* 2015. 30 Jun. 2017.

http://mag.ispo.com/2015/01/90-percent-of-all-purchasing-decisions-are-made-subconsciously/?lang=en.
5. 1 Peter 3:3-4, NLT.
6. Stephen Covey. *The 7 Habits of Highly Effective People: Powerful Lessons in Personal Change.* (New York: Fireside, 1989), 93.
7. 1 Timothy 6:8, NLT.
8. Proverb 15:22, NLT.
9. Proverbs 19:20, NLT.
10. Luke 6:31, NLT.
11. Stephen Covey. *The 7 Habits of Highly Effective People: Powerful Lessons in Personal Change.* (New York: Fireside, 1989), 213.

Chapter Six
1. "Retirement in America: Time to rethink and retool." PwC. 2021. 15 Sep. 2021. https://www.pwc.com/us/en/industries/asset-wealth-management/assets/pwc-retirement-in-america-rethink-retool.pdf.
2. Alvin D. Hall. *Getting Started in Mutual Funds.* (New Jersey: Wiley, 2011), 49-54.
3. Ibid.
4. "Beta." Investopedia. 30 Jun. 2017. http://www.investopedia.com/terms/s/smart-beta-etf.asp.
5. "Enron Fast Facts." *CNN.* 27 Apr. 2017. 30 Jun. 2017. http://www.cnn.com/2013/07/02/us/enron-fast-facts/.
6. Ibid.
7. "Individual Retirement Arrangements (IRA)." *Internal Revenue Service.* 20 Aug. 2021. 16 Sep. 2021. https://www.irs.gov/retirement-plans/individual-retirement-arrangements-iras.
8. "Traditional and Roth IRAs." *Internal Revenue Service.* 26 Jun. 2017. 22 Sep. 2021. https://www.irs.gov/retirement-plans/traditional-and-roth-iras.
9. Ibid.
10. United States. Dept. of the Treasury. "Contributions to Individual Retirement Arrangements (IRAs)." Washington: US Dept. of the Treasury, 2020.
11. United States. Dept. of the Treasury. "Distributions from Individual Retirement Arrangements (IRAs)." Washington: US Dept. of the Treasury, 2020.
12. United States. Dept. of the Treasury. "Retirement Plans for Small Business (SEP, SIMPLE, And Qualified Plans)." Washington: US Dept. of the Treasury, 2020.
13. Ibid.
14. United States. Dept. of the Treasury. "Pension and Annuity Income." Washington:

US Dept. of the Treasury, 2020.
15. United States. Dept. of the Treasury. "Tax-
Sheltered Annuity Plans (403(b) Plans:
For Employees of Public Schools and Certain Tax-
Exempt Organizations."
Washington: US Dept. of the Treasury, 2020 and 2021.
16. United States. Dept. of the Treasury. "Retirement
Plans for Small Business (SEP,
SIMPLE, and Qualified Plans)." Washington: US Dept. of
the Treasury, 2020.
17. United States. Military. *Thrift Savings Plan.* 27 Oct. 2020 30 Sep.
2021. http://www.military.com/benefits/military-pay/thrift-savings-
plan.html#top.

Chapter Seven

1. I used $2,000 invested for eighteen years invested at a 12% interest
rate. The ESA will be invested in stock mutual funds.
2. United States. Dept. of the Treasury. "Tax Benefits for Education."
Washington: US Dept. of the Treasury, 2020.
3. Federal Reserve Bank of New York. "Quarterly Report on Household
Debt and Credit." Aug. 2021. 22 Sep. 2021.
https://www.newyorkfed.org/medialibrary/interactives/householdcredit
/data/pdf/HHDC_2021Q2.pdf.
4. United States. Dept. of the Treasury. "Tax Benefits for Education."
Washington: US Dept. of the Treasury, 2020.
5. Ibid.
6. Kate Stalter and Emma Kerr. "The Ultimate Guide to Understanding
529 College Savings Plans." *U.S. News & World Report.*
2 Sep. 2021. 22 Sep. 2021. https://money.usnews.com/529s.
7. Ibid.
8. United States. Dept. of Education. *Average undergraduate tuition and
fees and room and board rates charged for full-time students in degree
granting postsecondary institutions.* Washington: US Dept. of Education,
2019.
https://nces.ed.gov/programs/digest/d19/tables/dt19_330.20.asp?curre
nt=yes.
9. Emma Kerr. "The Pros and Cons of
Working While in College." *U.S. News and
World Report.* 30 Dec. 2020. 22 Sep. 2021.
https://www.usnews.com/education/best-colleges/paying-for-
college/articles/weighing-the-pros-and-cons-of-working-while-in-college.
10. Quoctrung Bui. "Hidden Side of the College Dream:
Mediocre Graduation Rates."

The New York Times. 1 Jun. 2016. 15 Jun. 2017.
https://www.nytimes.com/2016/06/02/upshot/why-college-students-drop-out-follow-the-dollars.html?_r=0.

Chapter Eight
1. *FHA Home Loans 101: An Easy Reference Guide.* 1 Aug. 2017. Federal Housing Administration. 29 Sep. 2021. https://www.fha.com/.
2. Erik J. Martin. "Is a VA loan the best option? Pros, cons, and alternatives to consider." *Bank Rate.* 28 Sep. 2021. 29 Sep. 2021. https://www.bankrate.com/mortgages/va-loan-pros-cons/.
3. "What is a Conventional Loan?" *Rocket Mortgage. 10* Sep. 2021. 1 Oct. 2021. https://www.rocketmortgage.com/learn/conventional-mortgage.
4. Ibid.
5. "Balloon Mortgage Calculator." 1 Oct. 2021. http://www.bankrate.com/calculators/mortgages/balloon-home-mortgage-calculator.aspx#ixzz4ZB5h7UeE.
6. Amy Fontinelle. "Reverse Mortgage." *Investopedia.* 31 May 2021. 1 Oct. 2021. https://www.investopedia.com/mortgage/reverse-mortgage/.
7. Adam Hayes. "Title Insurance." *Investopedia.* 10 Sep. 2021. 1 Oct. 2021 https://www.investopedia.com/terms/t/title_insurance.asp
8. Laura Agadoni. "Why Does Waterfront Property Cost More?" *SF Gate.* 11 Jun. 2018. 10 Sep. 2021. https://homeguides.sfgate.com/waterfront-property-cost-more-34701.html.
9. Ibid.
10. "Credit Basics: What's in my FICO Scores?" *My FICO.* Fair Isaac Corporation. 1 Oct. 2021. http://www.myfico.com/credit-education/whats-in-your-credit-score/.
11. "What is Underwriting?" *Investopedia.* 21 Jul. 2019. 1 Oct. 2021. http://www.investopedia.com/video/play/underwriting/#ixzz4aPccEWrQ.
12. "No Score Loans." *Churchill Mortgage Corporation.* 3 Oct. 2021. https://www.churchillmortgage.com/No-Credit-Score-Manual-Underwriting.
13. Ibid.
14. Lawrence Yun. "2020 Profile of Home Buyers and Sellers." *National Association of Realtors®.* 11 Nov. 2020. 3 Oct. 2021. https://cdn.nar.realtor/sites/default/files/documents/2020-profile-of-home-buyers-and-sellers-11-11-2020.pdf.
15. Ibid.
16. Ibid.

Chapter Nine

1. Kimberly Amadeo. "Medical Bankruptcy and the Economy." *The Balance*. 30 Apr. 2021. 3 Oct. 2021. https://www.thebalance.com/medical-bankruptcy-statistics-4154729

2. Jeff Blyskal. "Is whole life insurance right for you?" *Consumer Reports*. 6 Apr. 2015. 3 Oct. 2021. http://www.consumerreports.org/cro/news/2015/04/is-whole-life-insurance-right-for-you/index.htm.

3. Julia Kagan. "Universal Life (UL) Insurance." *Investopedia*. 25 Jun. 2020. 3 Oct. 2021. http://www.investopedia.com/terms/u/universallife.asp?lgl=myfinance-layout.

4. Julia Kagan. "Variable Life Insurance." *Investopedia*. 3 Sep. 2020. 3 Oct. 2021. http://www.investopedia.com/terms/v/variablelifeinsurancepolicy.asp?lgl=myfinance-layout.

5. United States. Social Security Administration. *Disability Facts*. 3 Oct. 2021. https://www.ssa.gov/disabilityfacts/facts.html.

6. "Long-Term Care Insurance Facts – Data – Statistics – 2019 Report." *American Association for Long-Term Care Insurance*. Jan. 2019. 3 Oct. 2021 https://www.aaltci.org/long-term-care-insurance/learning-center/ltcfacts-2019.php.

7. Gayle Sato. "How Common Is Identity Theft?" *Experian*. 1 Jan. 2021. 3 Oct. 2021. https://www.experian.com/blogs/ask-experian/how-common-is-identity-theft/.

8. Kim Porter. "How Long Does It Take to Recover From Identity Theft?" *Norton Life Lock*. 24 Aug. 2017. 3 Oct. 2021. https://www.lifelock.com/learn-identity-theft-resources-how-long-does-it-take-to-recover-from-identity-theft.html.

Chapter Ten

1. 1 Timothy 6:8, NLT.

2. Philippians 3:13-14, NLT.

3. 1 Timothy 6:6, NLT.

4. Mark P. Cussen. "Average Net Worth of the 1%." *Investopedia*. 30 Aug. 2021. 3 Oct. 2021. https://www.investopedia.com/financial-edge/1212/average-net-worth-of-the-1.aspx.

5. Thomas J. Stanley, and William D. Danko. *The Millionaire Next Door: The Surprising Secrets of America's Wealthy*. Taylor Trade Publishing, 1996, p. 12.

6. Ibid.

7. Proverbs 13:4, NLT.
8. Proverbs 13:11, NLT.
9. "Discipline." *Dictionary.com Unabridged*. Random House, Inc. 4 Oct. 2021. https://www.dictionary.com/browse/discipline
10. Proverbs 12:1, NLT.
11. Thomas J. Stanley, and William D. Danko. *The Millionaire Next Door: The Surprising Secrets of America's Wealthy*. Taylor Trade Publishing, 1996, p. 12.
12. 1 Timothy 6: 10, NLT.
13. Proverbs 21:20, NLT.
14. Proverbs 13:22, NLT.
15. "UGMA/UTMA Accounts." *Franklin Templeton Investments*. 4 Oct. 2021. https://www.franklintempleton.com/accounts/account-services-support/opening-an-account/types-of-accounts
16. Julia Kagan. "Uniform Transfers t Minors Act (UTMA)." *Investopedia*. 20 Jul. 2021. 4 Oct. 2021. https://www.investopedia.com/terms/u/utma.asp
17. United States. General Services Administration. *Consumer Action Handbook*. Washington: US General Services Administration, 2016.
18. Ibid.

Chapter Eleven

1. Psalm 24:1, NLT.
2. Psalm 8:4-6, NLT.
3. Leviticus 27:30, NLT.
4. Malachi 3:10, NLT.
5. Deuteronomy 14:22-23, NLT.
6. Randy Alcorn. *The Treasure Principle: Unlocking the Secret of Joyful Giving*. (New York: Waterbrook, 2001), 63.
7. Malachi 3:8, NLT.
8. John 3:16, NLT.
9. Acts 20:35, NLT.

Chapter Twelve

1. "Hope". *Dictionary.com Unabridged*. Random House, Inc. 15 Jun. 2017. <Dictionary.com http://www.dictionary.com/browse/hope.
2. Jim Collins. *Good to Great: Why Some Companies Make the Leap...and Others Don't."* (New York: Harper Collins, 2001), 86.
3. Ephesians 2:10, NLT.
4. Galatians 5:13, NLT.